D1608739

82 REMSEN STREET

COMING OF AGE IN BROOKLYN HEIGHTS
Circa 1930~1940

ALICE DAVIDSON OUTWATER

82 Remsen Street, *Coming of Age in Brooklyn Heights*, Circa 1930-1940.

Copyright 2011 by Alice Davidson Outwater.

Cover photo courtesy of Mary A. Hampson.

Published by Wind Ridge Publishing, Inc.
P.O. Box 752
Shelburne, Vermont 05482

ISBN: 978-1-935922-04-9
Library of Congress: 2011931238

82 REMSEN STREET

COMING OF AGE IN BROOKLYN HEIGHTS
Circa 1930~1940

ALICE DAVIDSON OUTWATER

Published by Wind Ridge Publishing, Inc.
Shelburne, Vermont 05482

Contents

Dedication

To my beloved John, Mother and Father, and Louise Davidson Heyneman

Preface

I wrote these remembrances to honor Mother and Father, my siblings, and our wonderful Irish help who made our lives so comfortable. I did not want these memories of Brooklyn Heights to be lost or forgotten. I felt my children, grandchildren, and readers should have some impressions of the unique culture and changes that took place in the 1930s and 1940s, and I hoped it would help to make sense of the decades that followed. It was a remarkable place and time.

My family lived in Brooklyn Heights for nearly 100 years: my maternal grandparents, Grandfather and Grandmother Hooker, lived in 82 Remsen Street in a three-story double brownstone that was built in 1850. Grandfather Hooker bought the house in 1912. There was a garden in back and a carriage house beyond, which was originally used for the horses and groom.

My family lived across the street at 71 Remsen Street, and Father's mother, my Grandmother Hiles, lived next to us at 69 Remsen Street with her English companion, Auntie Pasco. When I was six years old, Grandfather and Grandmother Hooker died and our family moved into 82 Remsen Street.

I began writing these memoirs after Mother, Father, and my four older siblings, Jean, Sidney, Kitty, and Bob had died. I was the fifth child in our clan and a practiced and skilled observer, trying to make sense of daily life, keeping out of my older siblings' way, and bossing my younger sister Louise around. Louise and I were referred to as "bookends," in part because our next sibling closest in age was five years older than I. Louise's vivid memory filled in details of our childhood during endless phone conversations from my home in Vermont to hers in San Francisco. Each installment of these reminiscences was published originally in the *Brooklyn Heights Press*, and with each column Louise would eagerly comment, "I can't wait to hear what you say about me." I realized then how empty growing up would have been without Louise by my side, sharing dreams and concocting mischievous things to do.

Family histories often resemble each other, yet each family is distinctive. Father and Mother were essentially Victorian parents, not unusual in the 1930s. Mother was in charge of running the ten-bedroom, nine-bathroom, three-story house; Father worked in his law practice on Wall Street and managed all other affairs. Rules were clear and expected to be followed; manners were important and values were solid. It was assumed that we would treat others with fairness and dignity, uphold our end, and not ask for special favors. We were prompt at mealtimes and made our beds every morning before breakfast. In spite of living well, frivolity or excesses were frowned upon and education was the top priority. The girls would go to Vassar (although Jean went to Mount Holyoke), and the boys would go to Yale and Yale Law School. A summer was spent abroad before college with the Experiment in International Living and daughters were expected to work for a year after college and before marrying. Cousins and friends were welcome in our home and there was an unspoken duty to help extended family who might be floundering. Monthly stipends were arranged for retired help who had worked faithfully for us over the years. Mother and Father supported many community organizations, particularly educational ones, with time and talent. It was assumed we would all become good contributing citizens wherever we lived.

Despite the passage of more than 100 years, 82 Remsen Street still looks much the same and exudes the more formal grace and elegance of those earlier times. Now, although I am 82 years old, my childhood seems only a few hours ago. In many ways, life seemed simpler then; however, the hard work of those around us was a great part of what helped to make our lives so comfortable. As our circumstances were so privileged, I continue to feel humbled by the loyalty and good will of our household's help. I honor them all and will forever be grateful for their contributions to our family. This book also was written for you.

Hand-cut silhouette of Sidney, Bob, Alice (with kitten), Louise, Kitty, and Jean Davidson.

CHAPTER 1

Family and Household

MOTHER'S HATS

By the time I was born, Mother was forty-two years old. She was well suited to running our large family—two boys and four girls—and equally skilled at running the household and staff.

On the particular day I was born, our family was finishing Sunday dinner: Cottage pudding with chocolate sauce was about to be served. Mother announced to Father that she needed to get to the hospital *immediately* because of labor pains. Father, hesitant to leave the table before indulging in his favorite dessert, said, "Now Al, I just want to finish my dessert, then I'll take you down in the car. Surely you can wait a few more minutes." With that, he helped himself to an ample portion of pudding and sauce.

Mother abruptly left the table, barely stopped to put on her coat and hat, and started walking to the hospital. She hurried most of the way along Henry Street, staggering to lean against trees and wrought-iron fences until each new pain subsided. It was then Father finally arrived in the car and picked her up. I was born just after they rushed her into a delivery room of Long Island College Hospital.

My four older siblings had initiated Mother and Father into parenthood, a perk for my younger sister Louise and me. We were granted considerably more leeway and indulged in more than a few little shenanigans.

By the time I was born, Father's Wall Street law practice was well established and

The author's mother, Alice Hooker Davidson, as photographed in Remsen Street's conservatory on her wedding day.

we had enough live-in help to make life easier in a time when life was quite formal. Grandmother and Grandfather Hooker lived across the street and as their health began to fail, Mother attended to their needs too; she planned meals and hired household staff as well as nursing care.

Mother was born in 1889, a time when long dresses were worn and a hat and gloves were *de rigueur*. She loved hats and her children teased her that she must have been born wearing a hat. One rainy afternoon when no one was on the second floor and the maids were having tea in the kitchen, Louise and I thought we would amuse ourselves by trying on several of Mother's hats. I pulled out the folding mini-stepladder kept in the closet corner for such a purpose, climbed to the top step, and gingerly reached up to take a few boxes down. Louise was standing close by with her hands outstretched to receive them. But to our horror, I disengaged two stacks and six boxes tumbled off the shelf, bypassing Louise as they landed on the floor.

"Why didn't you catch them?" I scolded in my elder sister voice.

"But I tried; you just dumped them all on me. What could I do?" she replied nervously.

We panicked, not knowing how to get them back as I couldn't reach that high. We conferred with each other and seeing no other options, tore down to the basement to convince Bebe, our Irish nursemaid, to leave her tea and come to our rescue. Fortunately, she was amused and didn't reprimand us as she hurried up the two flights of stairs, entered the closet, mounted the stepladder, and neatly restacked the boxes. She hurried us down to the kitchen for hot cocoa and never did report our naughtiness.

I remember one moment in particular that typified my Mother's attachment to hats. She loved meeting ships at the waterfront when friends or family returned from Europe, and she would wave vigorously from the dock as the big ships pulled in, long before she could single out our family member or friend. On this occasion, Mother had gone down to the docks to greet her favorite fifteen-year-old niece Polly Davidson who was returning from a bicycle trip in England, Scotland, and France. Polly walked her bike down the gangplank with her summer supply of clothes in a knapsack on her back. Mother, always aware of the importance of proper dress, hugged her and said, "But Polly, where is your hat?"

"Oh, Aunt Alice, this was a bicycle trip and I didn't take one."

Mother couldn't believe such a breach of protocol. "You mean you were away seven weeks with no hat?"

Mother's favorite hats came from Miss Francoise on Madison Avenue. I never knew if they were actually more stylish or whether this fascinating woman simply imbued the hats with a certain mystique.

Miss Francoise was a tall woman of regal bearing, with beautiful long fingers suggesting a woman born into comfortable circumstances. Gesturing as she talked in her accented English, she fascinated me with her history. She had been brought up in the prosperous Bois de Boulogne section of Paris and her father was an *avocat*. Commissioned as a captain in World War I, he had later been killed in action. On her return home from secondary school at age eighteen, Miss Francoise found a bomb had demolished her house—her mother was buried in the rubble. Nearby cousins took her in, and she graduated from the école *superieure* the year of the Armistice. The devaluation of the franc wiped out the family savings and she now had to support herself.

Whether in Brooklyn Heights or traveling the world, Alice's mother was rarely seen without a hat. Here she is pictured at the pyramids in Egypt and relaxing at home.

Sewing was her only skill. As was customary in the French schools, the nuns had taught fine stitching and embroidery. She had excelled at delicate handwork and decided this was how she would earn her livelihood. Apprenticing herself to a Paris milliner, she showed flair for constructing and designing hats. She folded the horsehair with care, bending it to shape the hat, which she then covered with fabric. She selected various needles according to the thickness of the material, but always chose a slim needle for the crown. This intricate pattern of tiny stitches became her trademark.

In her mid-twenties, she married an older man of modest means, also in the millinery business, and they came to New York City to start a business. When her husband died of a heart attack, she had to fall back on her own resources. Again, she opened a millinery

shop and gradually began to prosper as the better stores recommended her to their customers. The small, narrow shop was cheerful and inviting with its green carpet. Facing the long mirrored wall, there was a modest vase of fresh flowers on the counter near a notebook of Parisian hats. Framed French prints of *Les Modes Parisiennes* showed women in fashionable outfits of the 1800s: long hooped dresses, gloved hands, and hats of every shape.

Mother would sit down in a chair, while Miss Francoise took the new hat from the model's head and carefully placed it on Mother without mussing her hair. Mother would lean forward toward the mirror for a closer look, puckering up her lips in her odd way. Then she would look from side to side trying to get a view of her profile. Miss Francoise would hand her a mirror, while

Alice's mother wore hats throughout her life; her hats became her crowning touch whenever she stepped out.

slightly tilting the hat to a modish angle. Mother would smile and nod, obviously pleased with the result. Miss Francoise would remove the hat, go behind the curtain, and return with a hatbox and the bill. She would then place the hat in the tissue paper squarely in the middle of the box, put on the lid, and pull out the maroon twisted satin cord. Mother would write a check and hand it to her.

Miss Francoise would accompany us to the door, waving her hands as she chatted, delighted that her newest creation was well received. She treated her customers with a certain formality; appointments were made in advance, so customers would not meet each other.

She ran the shop alone, serving one customer at a time. A few apprentice helpers sewed in the back room behind the curtain. It was rumored she had made hats for the Duchess of Windsor.

At Father's funeral, Mother sat in the front pew of the Unitarian Church on Brooklyn Heights. She was widowed at age 90 after 64 years of marriage. Mother sat like a queenly figure from an era long past. Sitting directly behind her, I struggled to anchor my pain by noticing the trivial details of her clothes: She wore her navy coat, a matching hat tilting smartly to the right, and a bright Hermes scarf tucked into her coat collar. I couldn't keep my eyes off the tiny stitching around the crown of the hat or the silver Georg Jensen hatpin that caught the light.

My confused mind reverted to the service: We were in the middle of a prayer. All I could see through my tears were the tiny stitches on the crown of the hat. I realized it was one that mother had carried home so excitedly from Miss Francoise years ago when I was just a young girl, holding her hand.

Snooping in the Closets and Drawers

My younger sister Louise and I kept track of everything on Mother's bureau top, regularly creeping into her and Father's bedroom when they were downstairs at dinner. We scanned the bureau to see if anything new had been placed there since our last visit. We unscrewed the jars of cream, sniffed the contents, put a small amount on our index finger, and carefully smeared it on our faces. We each took a perfume bottle, lifted out the stopper, and dabbed it daintily behind our ears.

Looking in the mirror we turned our heads to the right and then to the left as we had observed Mother doing. With that ritual completed, we tiptoed back to bed, pulled the sheets up under our chins while congratulating each other on how delicious we smelled.

I sometimes stood by Mother's side as she sat by her bureau and put on makeup. When she leaned toward the mirror I leaned too; as she flattened her lips to apply the lipstick evenly, I did too. Next, she powdered her nose so it didn't shine and only occasionally patted a bit of rouge on her cheeks. Sometimes she poofed a little powder on my nose.

Mother's third bureau drawer held her confounding undergarments. The corsets were a weird, long, cumbersome apparatus with an attached bra. They wrapped around the body and had to be laced up to hold in the flesh. The bone supports in front kept

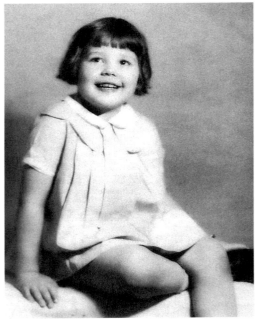

Who would have thought this innocent faced-child was capable of carrying out many mischievous plans? Photograph of author as a young child.

the torso straight, and dangling garters secured stockings.

Louise and I were ambivalent about the corsets: "I'm never going to wear one of those awful things," Louise declared. The pile in the drawer to the right was made up of white underdrawers that resembled baggy gym pants. These were pulled up over the corset. Next to that rested a stack of stockings, "Hole proof Hosiery," of lusterized lisle and pure silk for evening.

Souvenirs and gifts from the Davidson's travels abroad were always tucked away in a bureau drawer for safekeeping. Author's Note: On the island of Re off Pago Pago in the South Pacific, a native hat for Mother is de rigueur. Carried aloft a wooden-pole litter in Asia, Mother's hat provided relief from the sun.

The corset imposed a flattened look to the body; a pointy bosom would have been sexually suggestive. I remember trips to the corset shop off Lexington Avenue in New York. It was a narrow, uninteresting store where Miss Tighter always greeted us with a tape measure dangling from her neck. Miss Tighter looked like a dreary bird that had spent her life making these strange items; the effort seemed to have sapped her energy. Louise and I giggled about her name and agreed it was well suited to her trade. We recited our secret rhyme: "Oh, Miss Tighter, you look brighter as you pull those dreadful laces tighter."

Mother would disappear into the tiny dressing room behind a white curtain and we could hear murmurs about the uplift, which would reveal a faint outline of her attractive bosom. It all seemed so silly and mysterious to me.

One rainy afternoon my younger sister Louise and I grew bored playing Parcheesi and pick-up sticks and sniffed about for a bit of mischief. We thought everyone was out except for the maids having tea in the basement.

"Oh, Louise, let's go snoop through those drawers in Mother's highboy and see what she's stashed away for gifts," I suggested.

"I don't know, Ali, sometimes these ideas of yours get us in big trouble," my younger sister responded as she accompanied me upstairs.

It took both of us to pull out the two heavy drawers from the highboy, and plop them on Father's bed. Next, we tidily lifted all the contents onto the bedspread, methodically selecting our favorites for our own pile. We became giddy thinking this stash might be ours—until we heard the downstairs front door open, followed by footsteps on the stairs. There was no way we could jam so many items back into the drawers and replace them in the highboy; so, it was either hide under the bed or confess how nosy we had been.

Mother opened her bedroom door suspecting we were up to something. She stood there for what seemed an eternity gazing in amazement at the display on the bed. We held our breath and didn't move. Then to our amazement, she began to laugh. Mother had forgotten how packed the drawers were. Instead of scolding us, she seemed to appreciate our curiosity and said we could each choose one item for ourselves. This put me in a real dilemma; I was not thinking just *one* item for myself, but dozens. Although, of course, Louise and I were relieved she found our afternoon antics amusing.

I chose a wooden whistle made by natives in Java where a cruise ship had stopped on a trip to Indonesia. The whistle had a carved decoration on the side and made a lovely, soft, almost musical sound when I blew. I imagined it would be useful to summon Louise if I needed her. Then we carefully placed everything back in the drawers and Mother kindly helped us carry them to the highboy. "We'll never do this again without your permission," we earnestly assured her.

If Mother and Father were out for the evening, Louise and I would investigate the closets. Father's clothes were not particularly interesting: dark suits, pants hanging solemnly in precise rows. Next to them, jackets hung over weskits on wooden hangers. I preferred the feel of his tuxedo jackets with the finer wool and satin collars. The tailcoats looked like costumes, cut shorter in front with a V on both sides and long tails flapping behind.

His shoes were so highly shined we could even see our faces reflected, especially in the patent leather ones for evening. They were arranged in pairs stuffed with bulky wooden shoetrees. He was never without his gold watch chain tucked in the little front pocket of his pants, even for his long walk across Brooklyn Bridge to Wall Street. On a warm spring evening, my father might take off his jacket in the house, leaving him in his white or blue Brooks Brothers' shirt with its stiffly starched collar.

Mother's closet held her evening clothes and that was a different matter altogether: a whole row of dresses carefully hung on padded satin hangers was kept in the back of the closet. Short individual cloth covers protected them against dust. Beaded and embroidered evening purses wrapped in tissue paper resided on the shelf above. There were gowns for Boston Symphony concerts, for dinner dances, Rembrandt or Iphetonga Club evenings, weddings, and gala celebrations with friends. These were beautiful gowns made by Mother's French dressmaker in New York with elegant fabrics: luxurious satins, heavy silks, floating chiffons, laces from Italy or China. Mother's gowns were apt to be made of lace over a taffeta lining of gorgeous blues and greens. Some were short sleeved with a matching jacket. Some were floor length and others were three-quarter length showing a saucy bit of her ankle. A black velvet cape and a mink jacket hung to one side. Colorful satin shoes as well as silver and gold leather ones with stylish small heels perched on the shoe rack.

Louise and I loved to squeeze in the closet together between Mother's dresses to feel the soft materials against our skin. Then we would close our eyes and pretend that we were grown-up ladies going to fancy parties. My favorite was a daring off-the-shoulder fire engine red taffeta dress with a small ruffle at the hem from Saks Fifth Avenue. Mother admitted she had bought it in a rare giddy moment.

When dressed up Mother and Father seemed transformed, even their voices were lighter and gayer as we watched them greet guests at our parties. Before leaving for an evening out, Mother would quietly open the door to our bedroom and bend down to kiss Louise and me, careful that her string of pearls or crystal beads were not entangled in our hair. I could sense the flutter of anticipation as she turned to go, leaving behind a delicious cloud of French perfume. We could hear her pausing at the top of the stairs as she descended with a light step. "Sid, I've just heard the girls' prayers and I'm coming."

Sometimes Louise and I snuck out of bed for a last magical glimpse of them. We peered over the banister to see Father, dapper in his tails, black overcoat with a white silk scarf tucked in around his neck. He tipped his top hat to Bessie, our downstairs maid, and tenderly took Mother's arm as they went through the front door.

Forty-six years later, after Mother had died, my older sister Kitty and I were going through Mother's closet to dispose of her clothes. There in the very back of the closet was the favorite red taffeta dress still as rustling and whimsical as the first night she had worn it. A faint whiff of the French perfume still clung to it. I turned and looked behind me expecting to see Father waiting for her in his top hat and tails.

A Tight Squeeze at Saks

In this era, mothers dressed as adults: Dresses were of a prescribed length with nothing falling above the knee. Women did not wear pants, suggestive tops, or tight-fitting sweaters. On the street, hats and gloves were worn. Ball gowns and eveningwear allowed for more creativity—young debutantes' shoulders could be bare and skirts could swirl. Mothers never used eyeliner because this was suggestive of women in the theater or films, who supposedly were another breed with questionable morals. Of course, there were night creams and day creams to keep the skin moist, and expensive lotions in small jars that promised to smooth out wrinkles. Perfumes were packaged in delightful boxes that held fancy bottles, always with a glass stopper that might have a small figure on top. These bottles were artworks in themselves.

In the 1930s, boutiques were rare. Destination shopping was defined by distinctive department stores where you could find everything under one roof and ladies always dressed up to go shopping. They wore a skirt that went below the knees, blouse and jacket, stockings, street shoes, hat and gloves. All this attire did make it tiresome if you were trying on dresses because there was so much to take off. However, some consolation could be found in that you didn't have to carry all your purchases home; the store delivery truck brought them right to your house that same

The author and her sister Louise flank a pony while wearing outfits purchased at Best & Co.

day, or at the latest, the following one.

Saks Fifth Avenue, with its handsome interior, thrilled me. The elevators were operated by men or women smartly dressed in uniforms with brass buttons, small hats, and gloves. At each stop, they announced in a singsong voice, "Third floor: evening gowns, cocktail dresses, fur salon, and designers' hats."

On the first floor, the cosmetic counters featured pretty women in white smocks who leaned across the counter to spray the newest perfume on your hand or directed you to the

Alice with Mother and little sister Louise.

bright lipsticks. Their smooth, flawless complexions attested to the magic of the creams. These luxury items also suggested glamour, a subtle encouragement for shoppers to spend money freely as they mounted the wooden escalators to the more expensive floors. In the earlier era of horses and carriages, the perfume counters were strategically placed near the door to keep the foul street smells of manure out of the store.

Much to my disappointment we never lingered at the cosmetic counters because Mother did not fuss over her face; she used only a day cream, a puff of powder, and lipstick. I wished she would update herself: even my sister's college friends arrived for the night with their intriguing flowered zip-up makeup cases. These contained eye shadow and mascara in various shades that transformed them into mysterious creatures. My younger sister Louise and I loved watching them peer into the

mirror as they applied these unfamiliar beauty touches.

Mother had one friend, Mrs. Moore, who wore heavy eye shadow, rouge, and bright lipstick when we saw her shopping on Montague Street. I wondered if she too kept everything in a little flowered zip-up case on her bureau. She looked stylish if a bit overdone with her bobbed hairstyle. Her flowing capes over long swirly skirts were associated more with eveningwear than daytime errands. Mother said she was theatrical and played parts in the community theater. It seemed odd to me that her husband was a judge, a handsome man, but very proper and formal. He sat in court all day in his somber black robes dealing with solemn cases while she whirled about in these unusual outfits.

Saks Fifth Avenue was considered "tony" for its fashions and Mother checked there for the occasional cashmere sweater, evening gown, or Italian shoes. One day she planned to take a quick look at the evening gowns but not try on anything; however, she became enthralled with an emerald green beauty and couldn't resist seeing if it fit.

As Louise accompanied Mother to the dressing room, I searched out the ladies room. Usually they resembled the dark underside of the city and Mother did not like us using them. But Saks had recently redone its bathrooms, which now smelled of perfume. We liked the sparkling mirrors, Kleenex boxes, small terry cloth towels piled in a row, and soft lighting.

That day I somehow locked myself in a stall and was unable to get out. I was the only one in the bathroom and couldn't budge the metal hook out of the round eye. I began to panic like a caged animal and prayed Mother and Louise wouldn't leave without me while they were caught in the excitement of the emerald gown and new fashions.

I soon realized that if I pounded on the door or called for help no one would hear me. The opening under the stall door was low. I wasn't sure I could squeeze out on my hands and knees with my heavy winter clothing. So I took off my woolen coat and hat, and then my skirt, and shoved them all out. Next, I got on all fours, and lying all the way down I began to slither under the door. My chin pressed on the tile floor, which was wet from all the ladies' galoshes on that snowy day. I tried to flatten myself into a skinny octopus and little by little worked my way to the other side. Just then, a stern looking saleswoman came in, shocked at what she found. She crossly said, "Whatever are you doing throwing clothes all over the floor and acting like a ragamuffin? Don't you realize *this is Saks Fifth Avenue*? I'm summoning the manager who will make it clear you must leave immediately."

I scrambled to yank on my clothes and hastily made my exit. I found Mother in the emerald chiffon gown, admiring herself in front of a three-way mirror. Two saleswomen were standing by, telling her how gorgeous she looked. Mother was hesitating about the purchase, as the gown was some hundred dollars and well beyond what she usually spent. "Oh, there you are," she commented as she glanced toward me over her shoulder, as if I was interrupting the mood. "We wondered what happened to you."

I began to explain, but my story didn't fit in with this scene. I decided to wait and share it with Louise after we had gone to bed that night. She seemed impressed and said, "Oh, Ali, you were so brave! I would have been terrified and just stood there and screamed and screamed for someone to rescue me."

FATHER AND THE DUKE OF BRENCHLEY

I don't remember any discussion about it. None of us had an inkling Father even liked dogs, when suddenly he announced that we would be getting one. I had never considered this a possibility because major concessions were made just to allow Louise and me to return from Maine one summer with our two coon cats. Upon reflection, his canine impulse seemed logical: an English bulldog, the Yale football team's mascot, would make Father the ultimate "Eli man" and in some mysterious way enhance his status. He was a proud alumnus, a graduate of the University and Law School, and a forty-year trustee.

To acquire the dog Father scoured the papers for weeks until he finally spotted an ad: "Greatly loved English Bulldog needs a good home due to the arrival of a third child. Trained and housebroken, one year old, gentle temperament. Championship papers."

Father and Sidney, my older brother, drove to New Jersey to see the dog. When they left, I deemed it unlikely they would return with one; we were a family who discussed things thoroughly. Nothing was done without consideration of all the ramifications.

However, late that afternoon in they walked with a beautiful tawny-colored English bulldog. Donning his new leash and collar, he was formally introduced to each of us. Our new family member was properly bowlegged, had a curly tail, and had an engaging creased face: rows of wrinkles were covered with soft fur. It wasn't too flattened or too pugnacious with those frightening teeth protruding over the lip like so many of his breed.

In this unfamiliar situation, he held back as if looking us over, but I knew immediately that he would be my dog even if I had to share him with Father. After all, I was the oldest child at home and known for being responsible. I doubted Louise, the youngest, would walk him regularly.

Father had already named him the Duke of Brenchley, which suited his royal manner. This was in honor of my English grandfather who had grown up in Brenchley, England.

Father and I soon fell into an easy routine sharing Duke's walks. I took him out for a ten-minute stroll before school; then afternoons I hurried home from Packer to exercise him with my friend Clare James who had a boxer, far taller than Duke. Father walked Duke following dinner, just before turning in for the night. I was touched by his willingness to do this after a long day at his Wall Street office; he seemed calmer as he returned. Bending down to unsnap Duke's leash, then patting his forehead, he would lead him to his basement room.

Accompanying them both one night, I noticed that he waited until Duke was settled on his blanket before switching off the light, then quietly shutting the door he murmured, only half to himself, "Sleep tight, old fellow, see you in the morning."

It was through Duke that I came to know Father, especially his devotion to Brooklyn Heights, the quiet streets with colorful names such as Cranberry and Pineapple, the abundant trees, and the houses with their 19th century architecture. Father often said, "It's a remarkable place to raise a family and I can reach Wall Street by foot, or in poor weather it's only a few subway stops away."

But most of all he loved the Brooklyn Bridge, built by the Roeblings and opened with tremendous fanfare in 1883. Its soaring towers and cables spanned the East River connecting us to New York. To out-of-town guests he often recited the story of the difficulties of blasting the rock and filling the towers. There was a toll in human lives from the bends, then called Caisson disease. The bridge was looked upon as a major feat of the time.

Most days Father strolled the bridge to his law office on Wall Street. He claimed the wooden footpath that ran over the center of the bridge was rare in New York. "The only other foot path I know of is at Coney Island. But this is easier on the feet, unlike the cement one there. I've never seen more than six people at a time on the bridge. The Staten Island ferry makes a wonderfully scenic trip but can't compare to this. That's always crowded, and besides, it costs a nickel."

One morning Father decided Duke should accompany him, so both could get their exercise. But Duke's return posed a

Duke, the English bulldog, graciously accepted the attention of one-year-old Christopher Wetmore Walker, oldest grandchild of Alice and Sidney W. Davidson.

problem…until Father realized he could send him home in a taxi. Everything was timed accordingly. Father and Duke would leave the house 7:15 a.m. Arriving at Wall Street, Father would hail a cab, give directions to the driver as Duke eagerly climbed in, positioning himself like a four-star general in the back seat. During the ride, he looked out the window and sniffed the breeze as his little ears flapped. I would watch for his return, run down the front stoop, and pay the cab driver. Then I would open the door and take Duke's leash while he reluctantly stepped down onto the curb. Duke seemed to sense the taxi rides were above the usual doggy pleasures.

This was an agreeable arrangement because I could gather my books and arrive at Packer on time. But I was bothered by Father's extravagance. My allowance was fifteen cents a week, which Father ceremoniously gave me, yet he paid far more to transport Duke home daily. As a family, we never took taxis; we rode buses or subways for trips around the city. The car, which was kept in the garage, was only taken out for special trips. Father often said, "Money was earned through hard work and therefore to be treated accordingly." We lived well, we had maids and we went to private schools, but extra expenditures in the luxury category were carefully examined.

During World War II, taxi fares increased and gas was short. Mother's stern disapproval at Father's profligate behavior concerning Duke's cab rides never influenced Father. I wondered if Mother wasn't secretly proud of him doing something so outrageous; however, one morning the taxi fare was ten dollars and Mother told the driver he must have driven Duke all over New York and she wouldn't pay that shocking amount.

Duke was a remarkable companion. He knew when I was sad or troubled and let me gently place my arms around his thick neck and bury my face in his wrinkled fur. Sometimes I cried and cried, leaving his fur all damp; when I whispered my secrets to him, his big head slightly nodded in agreement. He existed peacefully with the two coon cats that occasionally arched their backs and hissed, but more often, they all slept side by side. Duke became a member of the family and was on good terms with everyone. Mother said, "We look like Duke and belong to the same family, and we will eventually all have his wrinkles."

Duke brought out a concealed sweetness in Father, and I am grateful to have been privy to this quality. It made me feel close to this formal man who fumbled about expressing affectionate feelings toward his daughter. I treasured this spring and fall morning ritual around Duke and the taxi rides. Father continued his daily stroll across the Brooklyn Bridge with his colleagues and had a phenomenal forty-five year record. Duke probably could boast the most number of crossings for an English bulldog.

Barnum & Bailey Circus Thrills

The Barnum & Bailey circus was coming to town and Father had gotten tickets. We rarely missed a year; he loved the elephants and the general excitement of the circus. Our tickets were for Saturday afternoon, but first there was the Tuesday trip to Penn Station at 34th Street to watch the elephants unload from the railroad cars. Father, my sister Louise, and I joined hundreds of people who lined 8th Avenue as the elephants lumbered out of the baggage car one by one, carefully stepping down the wooden gangplank onto the cement. Their gray, wrinkled skin hung loosely on their frames as they planted their legs and huge toes firmly on the ground. Trainers with iron prods were by their sides in case they wandered down a side street, but the elephants seemed to know exactly what to do.

Each swayed into single file, swung out its trunk, and grasped the tail of the elephant in front. Interspersed among the immense creatures was an occasional baby, reaching up to catch an elder's tail, almost running to keep pace. Many flapped their enormous ears and I noticed how each elephant's individual ear was shaped. Some even had nicks along the edges as if there had been a fight and a piece had been bitten off. After being cramped in the railroad cars, the elephants seemed to enjoy their momentary freedom and basked in the admiration from the gaping onlookers. A few relieved themselves, depositing impressive steaming patties of dung on the street; others let loose splattering streams of urine.

This particular year the group consisted of twenty elephants, although in the past there had been as many as fifty participants. In smaller towns, they were used to haul wagons from the flatcars and to set up the tents. In India, Africa, and Southeast Asia elephants were traditionally trained to help with logging and the British army used them in combat in India.

The crowd was delighted to see this undulating mass of ponderous pachyderms; the largest weighed several tons. They carefully wound their way to Madison Square Garden. I felt awed and noticed everyone around me stood quietly in respect for these gigantic beasts. They seemed out of context among the tall New York buildings with cars passing by in the distance. Jumbo was the largest circus elephant ever known, measuring 11-feet in height, and weighing 6.6 tons in 1845. Today they all looked mammoth to me.

"Look at those tiny beady eyes," Louise whispered. "Don't do anything to annoy them…as you know an elephant never forgets." Then as the last elephant passed us, four giraffes ambled by two by two. Their faces looked rather haughty with their noses in the air and those funny rubbery lips. They towered over the crowd, almost 14-feet tall with long knobby legs that they somehow managed to coordinate into a graceful walk.

Their tawny skin was dotted with circular brown spots. This year, two babies—miniature versions of the elders—looked like oversized children's toys. The scene had a Noah's Ark flavor about it.

After the last of the animals left our sight, the street appeared curiously empty; the animals' presence was so out of place I wondered if I had really seen them at all. However, I soon was abruptly reminded: as we turned to find the car, I stepped into an elephant dropping and began to skid on the mushiness. Fortunately, Father quickly steadied me, so I didn't end up flopping into it and dirtying my coat. I stood on the curb edge, turning the sole of my shoe this way and that, trying to scrape the manure off, but the rancid odor remained. Despite rolling all four car windows down, we experienced quite a smelly drive home. Because of the mishap and strong stench from my shoe, Louise was allowed to sit in the front seat again, even though it was my turn. I failed to see what difference it made where the odor's source rode in the car.

Louise and I waited impatiently for Saturday, which was our circus day. When Barnum & Bailey day finally arrived, chaos reigned in Madison Square Garden, which held over twenty thousand people. Hawkers screamed to announce their wares of hot dogs, popcorn, and balloons. Father stepped out of the throng to buy us each a balloon; they bobbed above us as we tied the string around our fingers. Louise and I had hoped that he would later purchase us both a stick of pink cotton candy; but now, holding on to the balloon and licking the cotton candy was too complicated. I noticed some kids had live chameleons pinned on their dresses. The creatures were wiggling and turning the same color as the children's clothes. I noted the pin went right through the body of the animal—which seemed ghastly.

Louise and I were drawn into the pandemonium; we each held Father's hand tightly as the crowds pressed in on us. Smells of sweaty people, popcorn, animal dung, and sawdust wafted above this river of humanity. Louise and I strained to get a glimpse of what was in front.

Arrows pointed toward the tunnel to the sideshows. Though I was both fascinated and uneasy, I never wanted to miss them. Sideshows struck me as tacky and embarrassed me. On one platform, the Fat Woman strutted around in her skimpy bathing suit. She tapped her loose flesh while her partner the Fat Man wore a thong; his bulging buttocks fell in ripples of skin. The sign stated she weighed 400 pounds and he weighed 450. As they sat down their flesh spilled over the sides of their chairs. They waved to everyone as we passed and I could see Louise wincing at this spectacle.

Next to them were Tiny and Mrs. Tim, so small you could pick them up. They were dressed in formal outfits, he in a tuxedo and she in a long black dress with layers of lace. They held hands and smiled, then sat on their doll-house-sized chairs.

I hoped we would quickly pass by the two-headed man, the Siamese twins joined at the waist, as well as the man with tattoos all over his body including inside his ears and on his lips. They all struck me as macabre.

Farther down the row were two women from northern Thailand with coils of wire stretching their necks nearly a foot longer. They could hardly look to the right or left. The placard said two coils were put on when the girls reached six years of age; they were extended by a few coils each year. In their culture, this was a sign of beauty and necessary to be marriageable.

A man from an African tribe showed scars in patterns all over his face; his wife's ear lobes were pierced and pulled down so far they hung like long flaps. I wondered how much this hurt and why they would want to disfigure their bodies like this. I was not yet aware of what the different cultures considered as attractive attributes.

Gargantua, "the largest gorilla on earth," prowled abound his steel cage hamming it up with Mrs. Gargantua, Mademoiselle Toto, in the adjoining cage. He weighed 550 pounds, his waistline measured 76 inches, and he stood 5-feet 6-inches tall. When he was a baby shipping out from West Africa, a disgruntled seaman had thrown nitric acid in his face, leaving deep scars and a torn upper lip. Gargantua's long, hulky arms looked enormous.

Just as we finished our walk through the sideshows, we could hear the band in the distance as the hawkers called through megaphones urging us to our seats. At last—the circus was about to begin!

Louise, Father, and I climbed the bleachers and settled in our seats, licking our cotton candy. Father opened his Cracker Jacks and seemed especially delighted to find a surprise inside the box. He put it in his breast pocket for Mother. He opened his mouth wide and began pitching the Cracker Jacks in quickly like a clown. He looked so silly. Louise and I poked each other as we chuckled at him. The band played a combination of jazz and lively music that electrified the audience to a frenzy as the circus was about to begin.

As drums rolled the master of ceremonies burst through a curtained entrance. He sported polished black riding boots, jodhpur-type trousers, and a red frock coat trimmed in gold braid. Next, a parade of clowns meandered in with their big floppy feet, colorful baggy costumes, white made-up faces with huge smiles, and various silly hairdos. Some were blowing bubbles, one was pushing a baby carriage with a dog in it, and another was bouncing a ball…such unexpected, ridiculous combinations. A portly policeman roller-skated around, sounding his whistle and waving his truncheon. "Wouldn't that be the funniest thing to have him skating on Montague Street?" Louise whispered to me. We giggled and giggled and peeked sideways to see Father laughing too. Emmet Kelly with his wide sad mouth tickled everyone and commanded the most attention. He was the beloved one of the era, later to personify all clowns of that period.

Then the acts began. We tried to adjust to the enormity of the spectacle before us: three large performance rings, each with its own act, swirled into a kaleidoscope of activity. Energetic poodles dressed in tutus streaked about, changing places as they jumped back and forth on seesaws, and tossed each other in the air. The jugglers came next. I found myself dizzy watching the swirling forms who managed to catch and keep so many clubs dancing in the air.

They casually tossed them under their legs, over their shoulders, behind their backs, and to each other. Next, gorgeous horses thundered out. Riders in colorful spangled costumes bobbed up and down on their backs, shifting their feet to keep balance, while the horses methodically turned in formation. I didn't know which of the three rings to observe. I began to feel slightly bewildered, but knew that scarier acts were yet to come. A roar came up from the audience about an act in another ring that I had missed.

Soon most everyone focused on the lions in a round central cage. They sat on stools, the males with handsome manes, and all with tufted tails. We could hear the sharp crack of the trainer's whip as the lions leapt through hoops, some rimmed with fire. As the trainer turned to command another animal, the ones behind him would swat out a paw and growl. Danger lurked inside that cage. I remembered an article about a lion jumping on the trainer and maiming him; I

prayed this would not happen today.

The elephants marched out; some dressed in skirts, others in sailor hats. They balanced on rolling barrels, spun around, each holding a showgirl in its mouth, and performed the "long mount" when a second elephant places its feet on the back of the first and so on down the line. Two giraffes with their babies joined them with riders on their backs attired in spotted costumes.

After intermission, a small car tooted out and stopped. A clown opened the door and a clown came out…followed by another, and another, and another, until eighteen clowns stood in a row. I wondered how the clowns could possibly fit in that small space with their big feet and bulky costumes. The next thing I knew a telephone booth was wheeled out and more and more clowns poured out of it, as if they had been deflated and packed in a can.

The aerial acts always made me wince. Before the tightrope act began, two or three brightly dressed artists settled on a tiny wooden square looking like flies on a ceiling. Using a pole for balance one started to walk carefully across the wire, pausing after every few steps to regain his equilibrium until he reached the other side. Then two men mounted a bicycle and reached the opposite platform, usually wavering midpoint as if about to fall. I knew they were just warming up for the most nerve-wracking feats to come.

I did like watching the trapeze artists in their ballet-type slippers, tights, and close-fitting ornate shirts, as they nimbly climbed up the swinging rope ladders and stepped onto the platforms. What made me flinch was when one pushed off the platform, and then was caught by the wrists in midair by his counterpart. They hovered in space. One man executed a single somersault, and then the double and a half. I kept checking to be certain the safety net hung below. I could hardly bear to watch, and my neck was beginning to hurt from its unnatural tilted-backward position in craning to see.

All of a sudden, something happened. The trapeze artist missed catching the other man in mid-air. The crowd gasped as he plunged to the net below, bounced high after landing, and then lay still. Father half jumped up from his seat in concern, then slowly sat down looking our way to see that we were all right. For a moment, it was as if an electrical switch had flipped: the music stopped and no one breathed. Then the band frantically picked up as if nothing had gone wrong.

The next thing we knew, a screaming, recklessly driven ambulance by clown Emmet Kelly rushed out with ten clowns hanging onto its side waving. A doctor clown in a white coat and stethoscope seemed in charge. A stretcher was immediately taken out and the aerialist carefully lifted onto it, and then put in the ambulance. The vehicle tore off behind the curtain as the clowns hooted and yelled. A deathly quietness came over the crowd, which wondered whether this was part of the act or a serious injury. Louise and I sensed something had gone very wrong and we could hardly enjoy the remainder of the show. I grabbed her hand for comfort.

The final parade concluded the circus. Suddenly the lights were too bright, the hype too much and the music too loud. Louise and I could hardly clap.

BESSIE DEFENDS FATHER'S BACON

Mother interviewed twenty-five girls for the position of downstairs maid; the line stretched the length of Remsen Street. The wage was to be fifteen dollars a week including room and board, generous for the time. The person would have Thursday and Sunday afternoons off, and they could attend early Sunday Mass, returning before we came down for breakfast.

Bessie came to work for our family in 1936 when she was thirty and I was six years old. Grandfather and Grandmother Hooker had died, and we had moved across the street to what had been their home at 82 Remsen Street.

Bessie was of medium height, a tidy figure in her starched blue-striped uniform with white apron. Her brown hair was wavy; it later turned to gray and thinned considerably. She never lost the lilt in her speech or her Irish brogue. She had a long face that seemed both pensive and wise. Bessie's outstanding characteristics were her fairness, her dedication to our family, and her determination to do her best.

I loved Bessie as only a child could. She treated people equally and never favored one family member over another. I never tried to cut a deal with Bessie. Whatever the problem, she would suggest, "Oh, Miss Alice, you and Miss Louise need to settle that amongst yourselves," or "You must discuss that with your mother, she'll know what to do," or "I don't think your mother would approve of that." That was enough

to make me reconsider and pull back to centerline.

Bessie's domain was the upstairs pantry. She set the table and served the meals. The cook placed the hot dishes of food from the kitchen onto the dumbwaiter and one of the women would pull on the thick rope until the contents arrived in the pantry. Bessie washed dishes in the stainless steel pantry sink and then stacked them in the tall oak dining room cabinets. She also vacuumed and dusted the downstairs, dining room, conservatory with plants, large living room, and entry hall.

Bessie commanded respect from everyone just by being who she was. No one wanted to displease her. She rarely got in tiffs with the help, but I do remember her muttering under her breath, "Oh, she's a difficult one, that Miss Josephine, always wanting special attention."

At four o'clock, after changing into her black taffeta uniform, she served afternoon tea in the living room. On the silver tray, she placed the round, fluted teapot, Guernsey jug of hot water, the creamer and sugar dish, and porcelain teacups carefully arranged with teaspoons lined up beside them. Then she returned for the teacake or cookies.

Bessie was known to have a sharp, quick tongue when pushed too far. I once overheard her scolding the new cook who had forgotten Father's breakfast bacon. "Ye know Mr. Davidson *always* has bacon with

Bessie's domain was the upstairs pantry. She served meals in the dining room and afternoon tea in the living room.

his eggs and shouldn't be walking the Brooklyn Bridge to the office without it," chided Bessie in a brogue so broad I thought a third person had arrived in the kitchen.

I never tired of following Bessie around the house to assist her with chores or to visit. Bessie allowed me to help polish the silver in the pantry Wednesday mornings. She put an apron around my waist to protect my plaid skirt. Next, she took out the black container of Gorham silver polish, coated a cloth with pink paste, and vigorously rubbed the tines of the forks and handles of the knives and spoons. Then Bessie handed me the pieces to burnish with an old Turkish towel. I sat on a high stool next to her, chattering away about grade school, comforted by this weekly ritual.

Mother brought fresh flowers from the Fulton Fish Market on Fridays and Bessie created impressive artistic arrangements in crystal vases and placed them in the downstairs rooms. Every night she re-gathered all the vases, positioned them on the dumbwaiter, and walked downstairs to set them in the large refrigerator off the laundry room. The next morning she reversed the process. "They last a week longer this way and will save Mr. Davidson money. Oh, those long hours your father spends at the office with nary a complaint."

Bessie's room was on the top floor and I often peeked in. I guessed it resembled a convent room: a cross was hung above the white iron bed and a picture of Jesus was on the wall. A neatly folded blanket lay at the bottom of the smoothed white bedspread. A lace bureau scarf covered the top of the oak bureau. The only other furnishings were a bedside table with her rosary.

At times, Bessie would reminisce: "I remember my mother weeding the vegetable garden in Ireland and how proud she was of those gigantic potatoes. Her supply would feed us most of the winter… the thick stew she used to make and those lovely smells from the kitchen. She always had a pot of nourishing soup boiling on the stove." Then Bessie would stop and say no more.

Tears for an Irish Nursemaid

Louise and I held our nursemaid Bebe's hands as we approached Penny Bridge on Montague Terrace. We were going to count how many steps it took to reach the other side of the bridge. We each took two turns to be sure the count was accurate, and then Bebe did likewise, although her steps were longer than ours were.

We glanced across the East River to the buildings; Father was probably in his office at 2 Wall Street on the other side. Only two ferries were on the water. We sniffed the damp air, and Bebe told us to shield our face from the wind with our mittens.

Bebe seemed to appreciate these adventures as much as we did. She was caring and not too strict—but rules were rules and we knew we must not break them. She usually straightened out any infringements with us so little naughtiness was reported to Mother.

Just then, an Irish friend stopped to chat with Bebe. On Furman Street below, Louise and I saw men hustling about unloading cargo ships. The docks were out of bounds for us. As the two women visited, I enticed Louise to sneak down the hill toward the docks. When Bebe realized we had left, she came running after us and was angrier than I had ever seen her. She yanked us back to Montague Terrace, sat us down on a stoop, and explained how dangerous this could be. Her angry voice frightened Louise and me;

Louise, Bebe, and Alice photographed in a relaxed summer moment when Bebe's thick brown hair was worn down.

we certainly did not want Mother to learn about this. We never attempted to venture to the docks again.

Bebe had come from Ireland three years before. She told us tales of her small town and her large family. She had nursed her grandmother until she died in her ninety-first year. Times had been hard with few jobs; some days little food was in the house.

Even though she was an adult, Bebe felt her opportunities would be better in this

Alice and Louise's nursemaid, Bebe, was a reassuring presence for the two little girls.

"Oh, Bebe, you must love having the Hudson River nearby, then maybe Ireland doesn't seem so far away," I said enthusiastically. She nodded wistfully.

Bebe was of medium height, with a full figure. She had the most gorgeous dark brown hair that she braided and twirled in a bun in the back. My sister Louise had blond springy curls that everyone stopped to admire; I used to be annoyed by this until Bebe arrived and we realized my hair was like hers. After brushing my hair in the morning, Bebe helped me braid it. She never did things for us that we could not do ourselves. She would say in her Irish brogue, "Miss Alice, it's important you learn to do everything yourself so you can be independent when you grow up."

Then Bebe met Patrick, an Irish policeman who was raised in a town near hers in Ireland. He had been in her older brother's class and she'd had a crush on him, wishing he were exactly her age. He had arrived in New York several years earlier, and he had become well established in the police department. Bebe's Aunt Theresa and Uncle Sean had reintroduced them here.

We shared her excitement as she told us about him. How they would take the nickel ferry ride from New York to New Jersey, hold hands, and watch the full moon. "Oh, Miss Alice, it's truly a miracle to fall in love at my age."

Previously, Patrick had been married just a year when his wife and their baby both

country. Her mother wrote her two aunts and uncles in New York, who replied they would welcome and keep an eye on Bebe if she came. She saved some money from odd jobs and borrowed from her father to buy a third class ticket, then bravely took the steamship from Dublin. She said with her voice quivering, "Oh, how homesick I was for my own little town... green pastures and all the friendly people. No one knew who I was here, and I longed to see a familiar face. But then I came to live with your family and it's fine now."

died in childbirth, and after that experience, he never thought he could be happy again. Happily, however, Bebe and Patrick soon became engaged and set a wedding date for the following spring.

That spring she planned to leave us and prepare for the wedding. I made her do all our favorite walks for the last time; I often returned home feeling so dispirited I could hardly keep from crying. I wanted to be delighted for her, so I tried to hide my pain. Two days before Bebe left, Louise and I made oatcakes from an Irish recipe I had found. We had a tea party in the kitchen on Friday. Then she left on Saturday. Her tall, handsome Patrick came to carry her belongings to his car. I understood why she thought him so special.

I couldn't put into words how important she was to me. For nights, I tried to muffle my sobbing into my pillow so it wouldn't upset Louise. We were asked to her wedding and excitedly, we wore our new plaid taffeta dresses with big sashes. We even went to the reception and ate fancy dark chocolates with tangy peppermint fillings. Mother let us each have two.

Then we lost track of Bebe. As I braided my hair each morning, I wondered if she ever, ever thought of me. Two years later, after she had her first baby, she telephoned Mother to invite us for lunch. We walked up three flights of stairs to her little apartment, and I was surprised how bright and sunny it was. She hugged me warmly and kissed me on the forehead. She served us soup and egg sandwiches with mayonnaise just as she used to make at home. I was older now and could appreciate how proud Bebe was of her new situation.

She whispered to me that she had named her little girl Alice: "Now, Miss Alice, there are three of us with thick brown hair. I can't wait until hers is long enough to braid just like I used to do yours. You know I'll never forget you."

Eva's Espionage and Feisty Brigit

Meals were an occasion when I grew up in the 1930s. The food shopping and preparation required endless hours. Leaves were often added to the dining room table to accommodate our large family and its frequent guests. An Irish linen tablecloth signified a holiday meal or special occasion; some of these linens had belonged to our Grandmother and Grandfather Hooker. We used our Tiffany sterling silver with a mythological pattern for more formal Sunday noon dinners and when we hosted guests. I liked this cutlery the best because each utensil was substantial and elaborately engraved with pictures from Greek mythology. Glass finger bowls on a glass plate were always placed to each person's left. We each had our own silver napkin ring with our initials, positioned to the left of the place setting.

Informal suppers, breakfasts, and lunches meant using the plated flat silver, stamped with Mother's AHD monogram and placemats. The white linen ones were the fussiest: all spots showed and they wrinkled easily, which meant they had to be washed and ironed frequently. The sturdier Italian ones Mother had bought during a trip to Italy proved more practical. They had a pattern of animals, copied from St. Mark's Cathedral. This etiquette and reassuring rituals required the regular support and hard work of our dedicated household staff.

One spring however, Bessie left for Ireland to see her family. Mother called the agency to hire a temporary replacement. A charming pink-cheeked Irish girl named Brigit arrived with good references and seemed very willing. Brigit's previous employers did not live as formally as we did, and it took her a whole month to understand the intricacies of our rituals. Mother spent extra time explaining table settings to her, but she didn't quite grasp the smaller details. This was upsetting to Father, who did not want his routine altered in any fashion.

Brigit questioned why we used the long-stemmed Waterford crystal goblets (they were delicate to wash). Brigit liked to participate in our dinner conversation and she was known to correct Father about a fact as he proceeded with a story. She would ask why Father wanted all those refills of ice water from the silver pitcher. She forgot the knife sharpener one Sunday when he carved a large roast beef. Brigit became confused over which side to place the plate when serving. She felt it a waste of time to serve vegetables to each person and thought we should just pass the silver dish down the table.

One dinner, as she served the creamed spinach, she held the dish too high. Our guest misjudged, plopping the green gooey spinach on the white tablecloth instead of on her plate. At which point Brigit giggled and commented, "Ye missed, as I knew you would."

Most disrupting of all, instead of taking the dishes one by one when clearing the table, Brigit clattered a racket as she stacked the plates one on top of another and grabbed all the silver utensils in one hand. One time I was afraid she was going to scrape the contents from one plate to another right under Father's nose. When Mother corrected her, Brigit said her way was more efficient and faster. Father felt Brigit was gauche. I was nervous for her, assuming she understood the intricacies—but did not want to bother.

Brigit didn't have Bessie's talent with the flower arrangements and preferred to jam the long stems willy-nilly into the tall vases without trimming the bottom leaves or positioning them gracefully. Nor did she bother to change the water mid-week, so it became cloudy. All these were but small details—but in our meticulous household, they were considered important. Despite this, I rather liked Brigit's feistiness and admired her daring in questioning Father and giving advice to Mother on how to run our household.

I discovered that Brigit loved Irish music, and especially loved to dance the jig. She promised to teach Louise and me how to do it. She even had a phonograph record. So one afternoon we met her in the downstairs maids' living room where she put on the record and demonstrated the steps. She let down her red hair and wore her soft black leather dancing shoes with a multi-colored cotton skirt. Soon Louise and I were performing the intricate steps, lifting our feet high and prancing as we imitated her. I undid my long braids and whirled my hair around as Brigit did. Louise's hair was too curly and short to join in this fun gesture.

Suddenly the downstairs doorbell rang, and it was the Irish priest coming for his bimonthly visit. He looked especially serious—nothing light or jolly in his manner that afternoon.

Brigit quickly turned off the music and disappeared into the other room. She changed into her maid's uniform and pinned her russet silken hair back in a bun. Our laughter and fun were definitely too frivolous for such a visit. Brigit later told me she had skipped mass twice to meet her boyfriend instead, and she had not gone to confession. In addition, her boyfriend wasn't even Catholic. This was most unacceptable to the padre. Assessing the situation Nora, our cook, rushed to arrange and serve the tea and cookies while Louise and I scooted upstairs on the double. No way were we going to hang around a fuming Catholic priest.

Just as Louise and I were beginning to enjoy Brigit's high spirits, Bessie returned from her trip. Of course, I was thrilled to have her back, as were Mother and Father, but I did miss the youthful carelessness Brigit had interjected into our family life.

One other time a substitute cook arrived in September 1941 before World War II began. Eva was German and looked far too fancy for the kitchen, even in her maid's uniform. I could easily imagine her presiding over her own sumptuous dinner party. She did turn out excellent meals, ones that actually rivaled our Nora's. Her sauces were tasty and she even remembered to heat the dinner plates for Father. Mother found her satisfactory but felt strangely uncomfortable with her.

The evenings when Mother and Father were out, Eva quietly came down from her third floor bedroom and played the piano for an hour or two: Beethoven sonatas, Bach, Mozart, all the classics with her skilled fingers rippling through the difficult phrases. I was greatly impressed, having had music lessons for a few years and was still unable to read—much the less play—such advanced music. As I lay in bed listening to the melodic strains floating upstairs, I realized I never, ever would play that well.

Mysterious phone calls often summoned Eva, always men with German accents. Her voice would be hurried and muffled as she talked. She spoke in rapid German that I could not understand and it scared me. Posters in the subways warned of espionage and the war coming closer to New York. Troop ships departed from the nearby Navy Yard carrying our boys overseas. I didn't want anything to happen to any of my brothers, cousins, or Brooklyn Heights young men I knew.

Then one Thursday afternoon, Eva's day off, Mother met with a serious-looking man in a dark suit, who I later learned was from the FBI. Apparently, Eva was under surveillance. Mother never discussed this with Louise or me, but the next day she thanked Eva for her service, settled her wages, and said she would not be needed anymore.

The following morning Eva descended our front staircase looking stylish in a black suit, hat, leather gloves, and wearing sheer silk stockings. She appeared rather royal, stepping lightly down the oak staircase with suitcase in hand—as if she was going on a cruise. I intended to say good-bye but felt apprehensive and hid in the living room and peeked out. Eva moved with grace and straight posture as she reached out, opened the door with assurance, closed it, and left. I felt her mystery lingered long after she left, as I imagine it did with Mother too.

CHAPTER 2

Grandparents

Wayfaring Grandmother Hiles

My Grandmother Hiles was a most unlikely grandmother. She stood tall and was straight and thin with unruly gray hair to top off her otherwise statuesque form. Keen, penetrating eyes peered over the top of gold-framed, owly glasses. Her nose was beaklike, reminding me of an eagle. She stood for no nonsense and when she turned her attention to you, it was best for you to be certain your responses were thoughtful and clear.

When we were little, Mother always accompanied Louise and me next door to visit Grandmother Hiles and Auntie Pasco—it was too scary to go alone. The brownstone at 69 Remsen Street was dark and crowded with furniture from their trips to the Far East. Screens carved of teak from Thailand dominated, and the floor was covered with Oriental carpets galore. Each piece had its own story. Two pillars in one room had carpets wrapped about them as if the dragons woven into the rugs were climbing up the poles. Between the pillars squatted a rotund four-foot Buddha with an inscrutable look on his face.

I was ambivalent about the tiger rug from India with its gigantic head. It must have been a handsome animal when it was alive and prowling around the jungle. I wondered why anyone would have wanted to shoot him. His pelt with those vivid stripes felt so silky.

Chairs were draped with batik fabrics, and a stack of large pillows of similar material

Grandmother Hiles, born Carolin Wetmore in 1865, was an unusual and adventuresome grandmother.

with cording and fringes lolled in one of the room's corners. The living room puzzled me and seemed very foreign with its unusual choice of furniture and fabrics.

At the sound of the doorbell, the cockatoo always shrieked from its cage and wouldn't cease, as if insisting we leave immediately. Auntie Pasco would throw an embroidered cover over his cage and quiet him. "Now, Van Heems Kerk, no one's in danger, just calm down," she would admonish. They had gotten him in Surinam and given him the

Dutch name of the boat on which they had traveled.

His screeches served as a warning should any unwelcome person enter the room. Yet he did provide real protection: on command, he would fly at the intruder's face and bite viciously.

Auntie Pasco told us the story about their tramp steamer, tied up at the dock to load cargo, when an intruder crept into their cabin at night. "Van Heems get him!" she hissed. He flew from his cage and bit the burglar on the nose and he ran away screaming. The next morning the captain told them that the thief had a long knife, was looking for money, and might have stabbed them. I found this a frightening story and didn't want to be bitten on the nose, so I always checked that Van Heem's cage door was shut when Mother took me to visit.

Louise and I liked Poochie much better. He was a friendly fox terrier mutt who often leapt out from another room. We were fascinated because he was allowed to sleep on the beds and anywhere he pleased; his white fur was on everything. Grandmother accepted that casually, but was fussy that he had his cooked liver cut up just so, three times a week.

At teatime, a servant from India carried in the tea tray laden with cookies that were sometimes stale. He was dressed in a dhoti with the colorful material pulled up around his legs like a fancy diaper and his head wrapped like a sheik. Although the house was drafty, the cold did not seem to faze him. He padded silently about in his straw slippers looking out of place in this Remsen Street setting. His English was halting and spoken in a singsong rhythm but somehow he managed to communicate.

Grandmother Hiles had been widowed twice by the time she was thirty-five. She attended Mt. Holyoke College for two years, and then met Judge William Dean Davidson while visiting a cousin in Augusta, Georgia. He had been a drummer boy at age eleven in the Civil War on the Confederate side.

Grandmother Hiles was a beauty and Judge Davidson was smitten. The judge was determined to make her his bride in spite of the twenty-year age difference. She agreed reluctantly.

On the day of the wedding in her cousin's house in Warren, Pennsylvania, Grandmother sat sobbing in an upstairs bedroom not wanting to marry. Finally, her cousin persuaded her to descend the stairs in her lace wedding dress and the ceremony took place in the living room. The story seemed silly to me: Why would she agree to marry him and then change her mind, when she'd already had time to think about it?

They lived in Augusta and she had three sons—Douglas, Treat, and Sidney, my father. Judge Davidson died early leaving a trust fund for the boys' education and a modest inheritance for Grandmother.

Grandmother returned with the boys to her hometown in Pennsylvania. Douglas, Treat, and Sidney were promptly enrolled in Lawrenceville School: my father was ten years old. He must have felt shocked to be dumped at boarding school that young; Grandmother seemed heartless to do it. Some nights in bed, I wondered who would have tucked him in, heard his prayers, or comforted him when he cried. I knew Mother and Father would never send us away that young. But I didn't know how to ask Father about these very personal matters.

All three boys continued to Yale College, then Douglas to Yale Medical School, and Father to Yale Law School. They married and had their own families.

Two years later Grandmother met and married Richard Hiles, a lawyer and a true love match. She was said to have recaptured her sense of gaiety as they traveled together and shared similar interests until he died just two years later in 1903.

Grandmother immediately had a nervous breakdown and would not speak or eat until Rosa Pasco, an English nurse, was summoned. Miss Pasco admonished her, "Tell me what to pack. We're going to travel tomorrow." This marked the beginning of a fifty-year companionship filled with around-the-world adventures. Auntie Pasco, who was jolly and welcoming but entirely practical, handled the money and did the cooking and housekeeping when they didn't have servants. Grandmother simply went along.

The two women had to manage on scant resources, to which they easily adjusted. They were inveterate walkers, preferring the adventure of boarding tramp steamers to remote islands in the South Pacific and staying in villages, sometimes for a winter if they so fancied, renting a small house, embroidering curtains, and having a garden.

For about ten years, Grandmother and Auntie Pasco settled down in Brooklyn Heights, buying 69 Remsen Street next to us at 71 Remsen Street. The two ladies continued their routine of walking everywhere; they loved matinees on Broadway, setting out on foot across the Brooklyn Bridge and returning in the same fashion.

I remember these excursions: both women properly attired in their long dresses, hats, and gloves. They wore sturdy lace-up English leather shoes with a low heel. Each grasped a large furled man's umbrella, using it as a walking stick, and over the shoulder an ample handbag that held a pair of galoshes, should it rain. They never complained about the weather or their feet hurting. Sauntering back down Remsen Street after the theater, they looked as if they were strolling along a country lane. I thought these forays were splendid; no other women on the Heights seemed to enjoy walking that much.

Grandmother seemed more approachable outdoors; I could almost feel comfortable with her when we met on the street. Something about her changed when she was at home. In an odd way, she then blended into her house and seemed unfamiliar and spooky too. Her long, bony fingers, her gray skin, and her frizzled hair intimidated me. I never felt that she liked children. She didn't seem interested in us or seem to know what to say. I could never picture her holding and cuddling one of her baby boys.

During these years, Grandmother and Auntie Pasco took a hundred-mile walk around Cape Cod. I can hear Auntie Pasco in her English accent regaling everyone with her description of coming into Back Bay in Boston, "We were full of dust, looking seedy, and in need of lodging for the night. This woman was reluctant to rent us a room because all we had were our handbags over our shoulders and big umbrellas. So we suggested she telephone our bank." Apparently the clerk at the other end said, "Don't worry about Mrs. Hiles and Miss Pasco. They walk all over the world, but they'll definitely pay for their room." So they had a lovely night and both took long deep baths.

Two Travelers' Tales

On one pause between overseas jaunts, Grandmother Hiles and Auntie Pasco spent a whole summer with us at Sebec Lake in Maine. That was when they taught Louise and me how to embroider and knit. They were experts.

This was a serious endeavor, and we would meet at the appointed time on the rock ledges by the lake. Louise and I were excited at having them to ourselves and were surprised at their willingness. I especially enjoyed Grandmother without her cigarette and holder, which were prominent whenever she held forth with her travel tales. Here she was quieter and more approachable.

She and Auntie Pasco brought their ample sewing bags with wooden handles filled with extra materials for each of us. They supplied knitting needles that were comfortable for our small fingers, as well as thimbles in woven Chinese grass cases with snug lids that had a distinctive fresh smell. I still have the little gold-colored sewing scissors with a stork above the blades and the red satin domed pincushion with pigtailed Chinese figures positioned around the side.

First, we each sewed a round embroidery bag with two pearl buttons attached to the drawstrings in which to keep our tools. Next, we mastered the simple cross-stitch, and then progressed to using colors and appliqué. We learned different stitches and to follow complex patterns.

Much to our surprise, they were patient and good teachers, as if they felt it essential to pass on these skills. By the end of the summer, we had produced some credible handiwork. We were proud of the sweaters and hats we had knitted for our teddy bears.

Soon after that, in the 1930s, Grandmother Hiles and Auntie Pasco took off again for extended travels abroad, renting 69 Remsen Street, and later selling it. Intriguing letters in their spidery handwriting arrived regularly with colorful stamps affixed to the envelopes. Father often read them to us during after-dinner coffee in the living room. In the privacy of the family, I looked forward to her vivid descriptions of their adventures, which were so different from our scheduled routines.

Every three or four years Grandmother and Auntie Pasco returned to renew their visas and take a breather. By this time, Grandmother and Grandfather Hooker had died and our family had moved across the street to 82 Remsen Street.

The two women would blow in for prolonged stays of many weeks. Their large wooden steamer trunks with the hump tops held with leather straps would be brought to the guest room. Louise and I were amazed as attention was lavished on them and the household revolved around their extended visits: theater tickets were purchased; each afternoon meant special Ebinger cookies or treats for teatime; friends were invited regularly for tea or dinner; aunts, uncles,

Grandmother Hiles stands at the center of this 1944 photo in a boldly patterned dress. Next to her in a white dress and wide-brimmed hat is Rosa Pasco, Grandmother's companion for much of her life. The author, then Alice Davidson, stands on the other side of Hiles.

and cousins traveled distances to visit. Grandmother's stopovers brought constant fanfare.

By the end of the stay, Mother would be visibly tired, finding it far too lengthy. I became annoyed as they paid little attention to Louise and me, and it was as if all those tranquil hours learning to knit and sew in Maine never existed. They seemed oblivious that they might be causing any strain on the household staff, although Auntie Pasco, who was pragmatic, was more aware. But Father adored them and wanted their time with us to be special. Perhaps having seen so little of his mother growing up, he deemed this time with her was significant.

Both women were extraordinary raconteurs, never interrupting each other, but, as if on

cue, adding details to each other's stories. At times, they resembled a comedy team like Laurel and Hardy. Settling into the most comfortable living room chairs after dinner, Grandmother took out her long cigarette holder and adjusted the cigarette; smoke puffs were effortlessly timed to emphasize the punch lines of their stories.

One season they walked from India through the rhododendron forests into Lhasa, Tibet, and spent the winter in a monastery. They embroidered a tea cozy for every single monk, and when they left that spring, they presented dozens more to an Anglican Church for its annual bazaar. This I thought most imaginative and could picture the monks in their saffron robes carefully replacing the tea cozy on the teapots after pouring the tea.

They were still embroidering tea cozies decades later when they spent a winter in Bellingham, Washington; they gave one to my cousin Sam Davidson, an obstetrician, and his wife Barbara. Sam loved his tea and treasured this item from his grandmother. He insisted the cozy accompany them on their sails in the Straits of Juan de Fuca. One ill-fated breezy afternoon he was sitting on the deck drinking his tea, when the tea cozy blew into the ocean. Barbara reported later, "Sam was so determined to rescue that tea cozy I feared the boat would capsize in the rough seas. I can still see it bobbing in the distance until it sank. I hope the monks in Lhasa were luckier and they are still using theirs."

Grandmother Hiles delighted in telling one story from the 1920s when she and Auntie Pasco took a Dutch freighter up the Sampa River in New Guinea. A tribal chief, who had never seen a white woman, boarded their boat. As Grandmother Hiles told it, "Being in need of another wife, he promptly offered to buy Pasco in exchange for a pig. But of course, I refused his offer." At this, without fail, both threw back their heads, laughed and laughed, before finally inhaling from their cigarettes in the long holders of the time. The story seemed so unlikely to me—and yet it probably was true. I didn't understand how they could be so daring.

Some years later when the same story was told, the tribal chief was a headhunter, who offered a herd of pigs for Pasco. In this rendition, he wanted to add a white woman's scalp to his collection. At times like these, I noticed Mother was barely listening. I wondered if she thought they made this up or had heard it too many times. Yet, Grandmother told it so skillfully I became nervous until the end when she turned down the chief.

Hiles and Pasco, as the family called them, loved walking on the continent and in the Alps but were especially partial to taking rambles in England. The villages were close together and public paths crossed the farmers' fields. "At noon we often found a church open and would stretch out on the pews for a nice nap, hoping the vicar wouldn't come in and find us," Auntie Pasco recalled without the slightest remorse. Louise and I imagined the wooden pews would be rather hard and uncomfortable.

I never could imagine Mother or Father doing this sort of thing. Certainly, no one on the Heights lived as they did, and I found it embarrassing that Grandmother carried on in such a way and then told everyone about it. My parents' travels on cruises or scheduled trips were more dignified but lacked such excitement and color; taking tramp steamers was definitely not their style. I always felt Mother was rather disapproving while Father wavered between being uneasy over their capriciousness, and yet, reluctantly, he admired it.

The adventure they prized the most was seeing the digs of the famous archeologist

Wooley in Mesopotamia, who was uncovering early structures called ziggurats.

Women were not allowed to enter the country but that didn't stop Grandmother and Auntie Pasco. They colored their skin dark with beetle nuts, then donned caftans and cloth headdresses to pass as Arab men. We have a grainy movie showing them indistinguishable from the Arab men, laughing and bobbing their heads as if in a Charlie Chaplin skit and of course smoking cigarettes. I found this spooky and wondered how they would have escaped if the Arabs had kidnapped them; I knew Father would not have been amused at trying to rescue them.

When they reached their seventies, Father told them they were not traveling abroad again. He was afraid they would die in some remote spot where he would never find them. By this time, I had begun to savor their outrageous stories and thought Father strict to limit their travel.

So they lived their last years in small houses in Tryon, North Carolina, and Sharon, Connecticut, which seemed lighter and sunnier than 69 Remsen Street. Each had a garden filled with brightly colored flowers. Grandmother applied her lifelong love of architecture to rearranging the interiors. They embroidered and told their audacious life stories until the end.

Science, Magic, and an English Grandfather

When I was a five-year-old child, Grandfather Hooker loomed like a giant at 6-feet 6-inches tall with size fifteen black shoes that laced to the ankles. Even his beard and two-inch mustache seemed unusual. But his long, nimble fingers did unusual things: he would bend his great frame down to greet me, saying, "chtoccha chtoccha paka," then gently pluck a dime from a strand of my hair, or pull a quarter from the hem of my dress. He'd hold it between his thumb and forefinger with a look of amazement, remarking, "I wonder where this came from?" Then, as mysteriously as it appeared, the coin disappeared, always leaving me in utter astonishment.

I was irresistibly drawn by his charisma and always tried to anticipate the next surprise: sometimes a colorful silk handkerchief pulled from his jacket sleeve, then wadded up and stuffed into his ear or thrust into his mouth to chew and never to be seen again.

Only once can I remember having dinner with him and Grandmother Hooker at 82 Remsen Street (although Mother took us to their home regularly for daytime visits). That evening Grandfather took the butter fork and matter-of-factly flipped a butterball from the silver dish right onto the corner of his butter plate, next to the roll. It was so neat and quick, I wondered if I actually saw this peculiar happening or if my imagination was embellishing things. Grandfather grinned mischievously as my sister Louise and

Samuel Cox Hooker, who stood 6-feet 6-inches tall, is shown with his wife Mary, who was 5-feet 2-inches tall.

I exploded into giggles while Grandmother shot him a disapproving look for this piece of chicanery. Everyone else continued eating.

Born Samuel Cox Hooker on April 19, 1864, at Brenchley in the English county of Kent, my grandfather was the son of a respected architect, John Marshall Hooker, and Ellen Cox, whose father owned sugar plantations in British Guyana. Grandfather

Hooker grew up in the bucolic setting of Sevenoaks, in a modest house within walking distance of the ruins of Tunbridge Castle, which had been the home of family ancestors. Its soaring stone archway led into an open courtyard, flanked by two massive Norman towers. But the family fortune had been squandered away through extravagant living. The story went that the male servants and footmen were dressed in fancy red uniforms adorned with braid and 14-karat gold buttons. To a child it seemed a ridiculous way to spend money.

As a youngster, Grandfather had hoped to practice magic professionally. I remember a frayed poster announcing his performance at age sixteen in a local establishment called The Lime Tree Coffee House in Brenchley. Although my great-grandfather was fascinated by his son's interest in magic, he urged him to get a scientific education. Young Hooker excelled in chemistry at the Government Science School in London and he continued his chemical studies at a prestigious institution in Munich, Germany, and earned his Ph.D. in two years.

Returning to London for post-doctoral work, he met an American, Mary Alice Owens. A feisty young lady pursuing her own advanced chemistry studies, she was the daughter of an Ohio banker and a schoolteacher mother. With her parents' permission, she had boarded a transatlantic boat to England in 1884. It must have been a courageous decision for a young woman of the period.

One evening as they stood side by side monitoring an experiment in the London lab, the night watchman came to check the room. As my mother delightedly recounted, "He found your 6-foot 6-inch Grandfather Hooker with his arm around 5-foot 2-inch Mary Alice Owens in her long black dress and high-collared blouse." Soon they were engaged, as she agreed to marry him if he would come to the States where opportunities were better. His uncle gave him three hundred dollars, and Grandfather followed his fiancée to Philadelphia.

Around 1913 my grandparents moved into 82 Remsen Street in Brooklyn Heights. It was a double-width brownstone with a garden and carriage house in back. By then they had four nearly adult children: Ellen, my mother Alice, William, and Samuel.

Since Grandfather loved Tudor houses, he worked with the architect Woodruff Leeming and local craftsmen to fashion the downstairs oak paneling, which continued up the wide stairway to the second floor. The paneling and fireplace details were similar to those of Knole Castle in England; the floors were laid with Turkish walnut and the wall sconces were bought in Sheffield, England. Grandfather traveled with his wife to Paris and London every few years to select fine oil paintings at expositions and salons. They furnished this house with great care.

The carriage house in back became his well-equipped chemistry laboratory; its slate counters were raised six inches higher than the standard to accommodate his

Remsen Street's carriage house Grandfather Hooker had a well-equipped chemistry laboratory with many shiny beakers suspended from the ceiling.

height. The second floor included a meeting room with sofa, armchairs, and a library. The bookcases eventually held many of his 21,000 volumes of books and periodicals and it was later deemed one of the most complete chemical libraries in the world.

One morning Grandfather invited me to his lab. I was enchanted to see Bunsen burners, flasks, and test-tube holders in careful arrangements on the slate counters. He lifted me up so I could look at the Petri dishes and peer into the beakers while he explained the processes, wanting me to grasp

his world. On the second floor were more counters, and rows of shiny beakers on twine hung overhead. I knew this was his grown-up playroom with everything so tidy and clean.

As a child, I understood nothing about his chemical experiments, but I sensed his fervor for what he was doing.

Whenever I would need inspiration, I'd picture him engrossed in his laboratory work. And I never spent a quarter without recalling Grandfather's endless supply, plucked from the hems of our dresses.

GRANDFATHER HOOKER TRIES TO THWART LOVE

Grandfather Hooker was a man of his times, and he therefore held a mid-Victorian attitude toward women. This is the story of how he tried to thwart the courtship of a woman who would become a favorite aunt of mine.

Grandfather's daughter Ellen (Nell), at the age of sixteen, had become smitten with Douglas Davidson when both families were visiting Chautauqua Lake, New York, for the cultural programs that were a popular attraction there. The year was 1903. The Hookers spent pleasant days in the company of a Mrs. Carolin Hiles, the twice-widowed mother of three boys, one of whom was Douglas.

Their days began at nine in the morning with a religious service and singing of hymns. The handsome open amphitheater accommodated five thousand from the Chautauqua community. Both young and old loved Chautauqua's variety of activities: swimming, canoeing, and sailing emanated from the boathouse on the edge of the lake. Tennis, badminton, and croquet were also popular. The two families eagerly partook in all of the offerings and that is where and when the romance began.

Nell and Douglas quickly became inseparable. They checked with each other first thing every morning to be sure they attended the same lecture; evenings they discreetly wandered off on shoreline walks, to talk and hold hands out of sight of the adults. Nell was enamored with his vision of service to others, his plans to attend medical school, and then to lead a missionary's life in China.

This intense friendship continued for the next two summers. Nell then went off to Smith College. There she delighted in the science courses, which she took as preparation to help Doug fulfill his dreams. "I love him so much I will happily follow him anywhere in the world," she told her younger sister Alice.

Nell returned to Philadelphia for Christmas vacation and excitedly reported to Grandfather Hooker about her semester: "I'm boarding with the Blake family in North Hampton because Smith does not have enough dormitory space. Dr. Blake has been so kind to me…he allows me to accompany him evenings on house calls to sick patients. He even lets me go in when he examines the patients. In the buggy he's careful to cover me with a buffalo robe so I won't get cold."

Grandfather stiffened and quickly thought this over. Later he had a talk with Nell: "Your mother and I have decided you will not be returning to Smith in January. I know what that Dr. Blake has in mind inviting you to accompany him in the horse and buggy. We must not allow this situation to continue. Instead you can attend Drexel Institute in Philadelphia and live at home."

Nell pleaded with him but he was adamant. Left no choice, she enrolled in cooking and embroidery classes at Drexel and later added some science courses.

Nell and Douglas continued their correspondence. Grandfather Hooker was becoming alarmed and expressed it: "My objection to this alliance has nothing to do with the Davidson young men. Your Mother and I are extremely fond of and admire Mrs. Hiles, their mother. Douglas is so fervent about this religion thing…I don't want my daughter Nell spending her life with heathens in China."

First Grandfather declared they were not to see each other for a year. He also imposed limits on their letters to each other, even specifying the size of the writing paper: Grandfather allowed them each to send a one-page letter every week. In their inventive way, Nell and Douglas wrote in the tiniest of letters using black ink, then turned the paper in the opposite direction and in red ink continued writing over the black ink. How could Grandfather object to that as they were staying within his rules?

In desperation, Grandfather announced that his daughters, Nell and Alice, would be going to Europe for an extended summer tour. Hannah Gray, a widowed friend, agreed to chaperone the girls. They would take the transatlantic ship to Liverpool, then the boat and train to Paris, and continue on to Italy. They would visit the important museums, cathedrals, and other sights considered essential on "The Grand Tour." My Grandfather allowed a longer stay in Paris so both girls could embellish their wardrobes with outfits made by French couturiers. Nell was far from overjoyed at

Ellen (Nell) Hooker and Douglas Davidson pose for a portrait in 1911.

this idea of being so far from Douglas but relished the opportunity to expand her boundaries.

Alice was definitely excited. All reports were that the journey was quite a success. It wasn't until I was grown that Mother wistfully recalled their trips to the Paris couturier for outfits. She remembered vividly, "Nell and I would enter the shops with Mrs. Gray. The couturiers always greeted Nell enthusiastically but never seemed to notice

The author's parents, Alice and Sidney Davidson, when Sidney was at Yale Law School.

me. One look at Nell with her presence, her tall shapely figure, and that swan neck… How they fluttered around her, pencil and paper in hand, as they whipped the tape measures back and forth. Finally, after they finished, they beckoned to me and with notably less enthusiasm took my measurements."

Much to Grandfather's dismay, this separation only increased Nell and Douglas' ardor. In one letter to Douglas, Nell wrote, "Hopefully Mama seems to be weakening and accepting our relationship." Grandfather had exhausted all means of discouraging the couple and at long last relented and told Nell on her twentieth birthday, "You have come of age and now can make your own decisions. Your Grandmother and I will give our blessings to your marriage to Douglas if that is what you want."

The couple was ecstatic.

After Nell finished her first year at the University of Pennsylvania Medical School, they were married. In 1912, Nell was twenty-three years old and Douglas was twenty-four. He transferred from Harvard Medical School to the University of Pennsylvania.

They rented a small apartment in Philadelphia and subsisted on a modest allowance. The following July their first son, Douglas, Jr., arrived. Because of Nell's long full dresses, none of the professors knew she was pregnant. She was able to take the summer off and then return to school in the fall. She ran home between classes to continue nursing the baby. The new parents were both so exhausted they went to bed at seven o'clock, leaving the nanny to take care of Douggie at night. Both of them rose at 4:30 a.m. every day to study.

Meanwhile Grandfather and Grandmother had moved to 82 Remsen Street in Brooklyn Heights. My mother Alice was asked to leave Vassar her sophomore year and return home to care for Douggie so Nell and Douglas could concentrate on their medical studies. Alice never returned to Vassar.

At the end of the semester, Nell's anatomy professor said he would exempt her from the final exam if she would give him her notebook with all her anatomy drawings. She did this, only later to appreciate his offer as the first real recognition of her artistic abilities. This talent strongly manifested itself by 1935 when she began to take art courses and win prizes.

Nell and Douglas graduated from medical school and passed their New York State Boards in 1913. True to their plan, following internships they embarked on a three-year missionary commitment with Yale-in-China. Grandfather Hooker had encouraged them in this endeavor, rather than their going all that way to try and "convert those poor Chinese people to a Western religion." He felt the young couple's modern medical skills might help alleviate the diseases among the Chinese, who lived in such poverty amid their dense population.

By then a second child had been born, a daughter Elizabeth (Betty). After carefully packing trunks laden with essentials for their long stay in China, the family of four climbed on the transcontinental railway bound for America's west coast and the ship to Shanghai.

In 1918, Alice married Douglas' brother Sidney as he entered Yale Law School. By then Grandfather Hooker had given up trying to steward his daughters' choices in husbands and welcomed a lifelong connection to the Hiles family. I am especially glad he did, since Sidney and Alice were my parents.

Grandfather Hooker and Houdini

Parties in the '30s and '40s often included games or entertainment. I remember one such night. The doorbell rang and the butler greeted the guests with obvious enthusiasm. All were magicians and members of The Society of American Magicians. They were dressed in overcoats, top hats, and tuxedos. Louise and I quickly noticed all of the men had long agile fingers and tricks up their sleeves.

Grandfather Hooker had also invited our family, which included my older brother Bob who had already mastered some magic tricks, as well as my older sister Kitty, who would participate in that evening's magic performance as a helper. My younger sister Louise and I wore brand-new blue-striped taffeta dresses with wide sashes at out waists. Grandfather knew it would be a unique evening for us. As it turned out, this performance for his peers was his last; he died later that year.

I remember the twenty-five or so guests moving gracefully, talking in clear and articulate voices, and standing poised as if on stage. Each held something in his hand like a deck of cards he was rifling while suggesting someone standing opposite "Pick one." Another magician was throwing rubber balls in the air, then squeezing three into one ear and taking five out the opposite ear. "Look over there," Louise said, as we watched a magician stuff a red silk handkerchief up his right sleeve and pull out a series of multi-colored ones from the left sleeve. Across the room, another did some legerdemain with strings and knots.

Louise and I squealed in unison as one handsome magician reached down to pull a stack of dimes from our sashes. Then a short stout magician lifted his top hat from under his arm and pulled out a live rabbit; we petted its silky fur until it disappeared again. Everything seemed to move rather fast, as every magician demonstrated his newest sleight-of-hand on his friends and us.

John Mulholland was among the guests; he was becoming well known as a professional magician who lectured, wrote books, and performed all over the world. However, Houdini was also present that evening, and he was considered the most innovative of the group. Newspaper reporters eagerly followed his daredevil performances here and in Europe. An assistant would tie him up in ropes or chains, perhaps using locks or handcuffs. Before he attempted his escape, a few members of the audience would come up to test them.

Viewers' favorite was when Houdini was lowered into a tank of water on the stage. He had a stopwatch made especially in Glasgow—the largest stopwatch in the world—so people in the gallery could see the second hand creep around the dial as he struggled for his life. In a matter of minutes, he miraculously disengaged himself from the strangles and surfaced alive.

At 6-feet 6-inches tall, Grandfather towered over the group. Louise and I noticed the deference and affection they all showed him. There was much goodwill, laughter, and anticipation.

Energy was running high because these magicians had received the much-coveted invitation to Grandfather Hooker's performance of "Impossibilities and Miltiades III," the talk of the magic community in New York.

The guests enjoyed cocktails as they mingled about, and then chose their dinner from the buffet in the dining room. But there seemed to be an urgency to finish and get on with Grandfather's performance. Finally, after demitasses, chocolates, and liqueurs, the group filed through the conservatory, down the iron steps, through the garden, and into the carriage house. They proceeded to the second floor and into the small "theater" Grandfather had built for such occasions.

Rows of folding chairs faced four small tables; behind this hung maroon velvet curtains. The "stage" was lit brightly by hanging electric lights. The front row, just six feet from the tables, filled rapidly; the closer the magicians sat, the more they might surmise about how the tricks were done.

Grandfather had brought a magnificent large stuffed bear that had been used at Wanamaker's as a Christmas display. His body hair was all matted from children patting him. Grandfather had unceremoniously cut off his head and replaced the button eyes

The April 1957 issue of a magazine for magicians led with a piece about an unexplained trick performed by Samuel Cox Hooker, the author's maternal grandfather.

with glass ones, which gave the bear a lifelike appearance. He named him Miltiades after an Athenian general.

There were four pedestal tables with round tops. One held Miltiades; on the others were a large glass bell jar and some equipment. My sister Kitty, John Mulholland, and Dr. Shirley L. Quimby were Grandfather's assistants behind the scenes. All were sworn to secrecy about the mechanics of the trick.

Twenty-one parts composed the performance, which lasted one hour. Everyone was given a program written on Grandfather Hooker's stationery with the title and short summary of each part.

Grandfather welcomed the audience. A deck of cards was divided into a number of piles and given to different spectators to be shuffled. Grandfather brought the houlette (tall bell jar) to the audience for close inspection before it was replaced on the table. The cards were then returned and put in the houlette.

Grandfather called upon the Queen of Hearts to greet the audience. The card rose, curtsied (by bobbing up and down), and danced (more bobbing) as the music box played offstage. Then the Queen was gently place on the edge of the table to serve as mistress of ceremonies.

Grandfather summoned the King of Spades and this card rose from the deck. Soon he stood on the table next to the Queen. Grandfather next beckoned the three Queens and as each rose, the ladies were given places to stand near the Queen of Hearts. The King of Spades watched, as if in reviews, as one card after another rose from the deck and returned into it. The Queen of

Hearts was the only one remaining on the table.

Grandfather told the audience, "The King of Spades is in love with the Queen of Hearts. Unfortunately the Queen has rejected him, so he has returned to the deck, disguised himself as the King of Diamonds, and will emerge to woo the Queen." The King of Diamonds emerged from the houlette but quickly returned. "She refused him," explained my Grandfather, and so he has materialized as the King of Hearts." This time the Queen accepted him. But as he returned to the deck to arrange the nuptials, the King of Spades forgot his disguise and came back as a spade. The Queen fainted and the King dropped back into the deck. After reviving, the Queen is so disillusioned she commits suicide by jumping off the table onto the floor... And the audience broke into applause.

Chapter 3

Peddlars and Purveyors

RAGMEN AND TINKERS

Many deliveries arrived at our Remsen Street doors in the 1930s. The milkman made his deliveries early in the morning. The dappled horse pulled the milk wagon diligently and waited patiently at each house. Mr. Gallagher jumped down from his seat, walked around to the side, and pushed the door of the wagon open. He carried six glass bottles in his wire container and placed them into the insulated box by the kitchen door. If the order needed to be changed, Nora left a note in the box so he could add or subtract from the usual amount.

The milk was thick with two inches of heavy cream settling at the top. Nora poured this into a separate pitcher and put it on the dumbwaiter for coffee or breakfast cereal. Bessie took it off and placed it on the dining room table. On cold winter mornings the cardboard top on the bottles froze. They resembled stovepipe hats like that of *The Cat in the Hat*.

Nora often requested a quart or two of heavy cream to add to the fish or meat. She also whipped cream and dropped dollops on the "floating island" and other desserts. Once a week a quart of chocolate milk was ordered, much to the delight of my sister Louise and me.

The mail was sorted in the 1891 Romanesque building with its tower and spiral at the corner of Johnson and Washington Streets. Our mailman then walked to the Remsen Street neighborhood with his bag bulging. He climbed up our stoop, stood by the front door, paused to shift his bag to his chest, then looked down and carefully checked our pile, which he thrust through the slot in the door. It landed with a plop in the entryway and was a source of anticipation as I always hoped there might be a letter for me. That was rare. Mr. O'Leary delivered mail twice a day during the week, once on Saturdays, and even on Christmas Eve so we would get our Christmas cards.

Another important person who came to the house was eighteen-year-old Peter Mahoney, who had just arrived from Ireland and delivered larger grocery orders from Reeves. In his awkward-looking cart with oversized wheels and tall wooden sides, Peter grabbed the high handles and pushed the cart from the back. Packed with individual brown bags of groceries, it must have been heavy to maneuver down the curbs to cross the streets. It could easily tip over if he wasn't careful, and I wondered if he had ever spilled all the contents on the sidewalk.

I could picture the eggs breaking free of their cartons then rolling about, and finally cracking all over the sidewalk. I imagined people avoiding the slippery yolks and hopping around the mess. The canned vegetables might merrily bounce all the way down Hicks Street slowing traffic before coming to a halt near a side street or a curb. I never asked if this had happened—but secretly, I wished to be witness to such a catastrophe.

Every month the ragman made his appearance on Remsen Street. He sat on his weathered wooden seat, whip in hand, bellowing his arrival to all, "Rags! Old rags!" He appeared shabbily dressed and his skinny horse expressed a sad and tired air. The horse was sway-backed and seemed to match the wagon with its shaky wheels; it always looked like it might collapse before they returned over the Brooklyn Bridge. A canvas feed bag swung back and forth underneath the rear of the wagon. It held oats for the horse's noontime meal.

The ragman also took newspapers, scrap metal, foil, pipes, and batteries. He rang the bell to the basement. Our cook, Nora, invariably had a pile of newspapers, along with old sheets, ready for him and stacked in a neat pile in the corner of the workshop. She would carry them out and hand them to him; he placed them in his cart and gave her a nod before going on to the next house. During World War II, some of my friend's brothers would carefully take the foil from chewing gum wrappers and cleverly roll it into a ball. When its diameter reached two or three inches, the ragman would offer them a few pennies for it.

The man who sharpened knives pulled his stone wheel behind him up our street. Nora was especially pleased to see him; she insisted that her knives be in the best possible shape to cut up the onions, carrots, and other vegetables. He positioned his wheel on the pavement, pressing his foot on the pedal like a spinning wheel. He carefully placed the knife's edge on the moving stone, which made a whirring noise as the sparks flew off. From time to time, he took the knife off and stroked the blade with his thumb to judge whether it was sharp enough. He was skilled in sharpening the length of the blade evenly, and above all, not nicking it.

The iceman made visits twice a week in his wagon that had a top on it. He wore a heavy rubber apron that went over his shoulder. He took out the ice grippers, gave a token brush to flake off the sawdust, and hoisted the block over his shoulder. He hurriedly carried it into the kitchen to be placed in the icebox. During a cold winter, the ice might be cut around Poughkeepsie on the Hudson River; otherwise, it would have come from farther north. The advent of refrigerators for widespread use in homes in the 1920s seemed like a miracle and cause for great rejoicing.

The pack peddler was of gypsy origin, and lived with the gypsy group under the Brooklyn Bridge. He brought a wagon full of ribbons, notions, and cheap jewelry and repaired saucepans during his travels. Nora would bring out our worn pots and pans for his tinkering. It was rumored that gypsies would steal children, and so we never ventured out to inspect his wares.

THE CLOCK MAN

Clocks fascinated my father. He was rarely without his heavy gold watch, attached to a chain and tucked into the small pocket of his vest. In the 1930s and 1940s, this was considered a necessary part of a gentleman's wardrobe and a sign of affluence.

Father taught us about the origin of clocks. The sun was primitive man's first timepiece; the shadows and their changes in size and shape throughout the day were observed to tell time. Next were sundials, which were positioned pointing toward the North Pole for accuracy and by the cast of the sun's shadow people could tell the time on sunny days. Later sundials were made so small that George Washington carried one in his pocket. The Greeks called their water clock a clepsydra (thief of water). This was a bowl filed with water to a certain mark; through a small aperture, it would empty at an even rate. It was particularly popular in Greece and Rome for timing the length of speeches. This concept amused Father as he thought lawyers talked too much, especially in court.

For centuries, clocks were made by hand and found only in the palaces of kings and homes of the wealthy. When the pendulum was used to regulate the clock's mechanism, that and the other working parts were put into tall ornamental wooden cases known as grandfather clocks, often standing 8-feet tall. Father acquired several of these over the years and on one trip brought back a grandmother's clock, which stood a mere 4-feet tall. I always thought it looked rather squat under the tall ceiling of the living room.

Father's Wall Street office was around the corner from Trinity Church, and he was partial to its tower clock built in the 18th century, which had to be wound by hand every night. Many European cities had at least one tower clock. The time was struck on a bell by two small figures called "jacks" so people who could not read the numbers on the dial could tell the time by counting the strike of bells.

Our house had three grandfather clocks, a smaller grandmother's clock, a ship's clock on the oak desk in the living room, a flywheel clock, two large-faced clocks, a wall clock in Mother and Father's bedroom as well as two bracket clocks on their bureaus and numerous others—all with chimes. The three-story double brownstone house at 82 Remsen Street absorbed the ticking sound. The chimes were all distinctive, some deep and throaty, others daintier and tinkling. Each had its own pitch and the sounds blended like the music in an orchestra.

Father admired fine antique clocks with good workmanship. He was especially drawn to English Act of Parliament clocks, which some thought incredibly ugly. I found them interesting with their outsized black or white faces and gold painted numerals with a small drop case for the pendulum. In 1797, William Pitt had levied a tax on clocks, which made having a small clock in one's home expensive. Therefore, Act of Parliament clocks were hung in taverns and prominent places in town squares. The way the populace circumvented this quirky rule delighted my father.

Occasionally a large wooden crate would arrive from London with Father's newest find, its history carefully documented on a thin piece of paper in spidery handwriting. If the clock needed overhauling, he would take it by taxi to the Antiquarian Clock Shop where they would carefully restore it to running order. Then a place would be found for it in the house or in his Wall Street law office.

Eventually Father felt overwhelmed by so many clocks and was determined to get them synchronized. It was vital to him that they all be accurate and chime at the same time. However, Father knew nothing about the mechanism of clocks, and became impatient when winding his own. So he found a Clock Man. Every Monday at 9 a.m. he arrived carrying a black bag, similar to a doctor's satchel, which held the tools of his trade.

I remember well the first time Mr. Cermak, a dark-haired courtly gentleman dressed in his black cutaway suit, lifted his bowler hat and bowed to Bessie, the Irish maid, as she opened the door. He looked almost scholarly with his wire-rimmed glasses, which he adjusted frequently as he worked. His hands were smooth and nimble. First, he checked the grandfather clock in the front hall, one of polished mahogany with a bonnet where a brass eagle sat on a ball. He reached up to get the key from the little shelf on the bonnet, carefully inserted it in the keyhole by the clock's face, and proceeded to wind it in a measured way. He unlocked the door on the case to check that the pendulums were swinging properly. Then putting the hour and minute hand on the number 12, he stepped back, tilting his head slightly, listening to the twelve-paced chimes as if he were testing their health.

Something did not please him, so he opened his black bag, took out a screwdriver-type tool, and made an adjustment. Then he had the chimes ring once more. Satisfied, he took out his pocket watch from his vest pocket and adjusted the minute and hour hands on the grandfather's clock to the correct time. Next he snapped shut his pocket watch, replacing it in his pocket. Closing and locking both the glass face and the door on the case, he then picked up his bag and proceeded to the ship's clock in the living room.

I trailed around after him for a bit, and soon became bored because the routine seemed the same with every clock. He silently concentrated on his work. Finished with the clocks on the first floor, he climbed the stairs to the second floor and made the rounds, then onto the third floor where just one clock ticked in the front bedroom. The whole procedure took two hours.

Mr. Cermak started down the wide oak staircase, his work completed. As all the clocks struck eleven in unison, he paused on the landing and cocked his head, a faint smile crossing his lips. Almost imperceptibly, he straightened up and continued down the last three steps. Bessie, signaled by the chiming, came out from the pantry to open the front door for him and they exchanged good-byes. He bowed and replaced his bowler hat. He said he would return the next Monday promptly at 9 a.m.

I always wondered where he lived and whether he had many clocks in his house. One year, returning from Vassar for vacation, I learned Mr. Cermak had retired. He had been replaced by a Romanian gentleman with the same quiet demeanor and an identical black bag in hand, who commuted from Coney Island. A few weeks later, I overheard a discussion with Father. The subway fare, which had remained a dime for years, was raised a nickel and he tentatively asked if Father could cover the fare. Father replied, "This is certainly unexpected, but I understand and will make an adjustment."

When Romanian gentleman died, he was replaced by a Bulgarian, then a Norwegian, and so on through the years. The clocks in our house always chimed together every hour, attended to every Monday morning by the Clock Man. As each man retired or died, another was found until Father himself died in his eighty-sixth year and mother in her ninety-sixth year. To my knowledge that was the first time the clocks stopped.

Cultural Mosaic on Montague Street

One bitterly cold winter day when Mother, my sister Louise, and I walked from our Remsen Street home and rounded Hicks Street corner onto Montague Street, we saw a crowd gathered on the sidewalk. I could hear some unfamiliar scratchy stringed music and I tugged on Mother's sleeve to investigate. It turned out to be a family of recently arrived immigrants from Estonia. The father played the fiddle while the young children, looking pale and thin in shabby, poorly-fitted clothes danced listlessly in scuffed high-buttoned shoes. A sadness and remoteness enveloped them as they mechanically smiled and performed the steps they had been taught.

Mother, obviously moved, gave us each a quarter to toss in the open violin case. Something seemed so terribly wrong with this scenario as only a block away my playmates were healthy and nicely dressed. In my innocent world, it never occurred to me to compare our large warm house to what must have been their terrible poverty. My small realm was so carefully defined and protected; I assumed everyone lived as we did. I was puzzled by what I saw but lacked the references or experience to help me deal with the information. I wondered whether the children went to school and who their friends might be.

In contrast, the cheery organ grinder from Sicily wore baggy trousers, a jacket with some buttons missing, and a cloth hat jauntily angled on his head. He followed the same route in the spring and fall, positioning himself opposite the St. George Hotel near the subway entrance. He roamed the neighborhood, arriving on Montague Street on Wednesdays and venturing to Clinton Street on Fridays.

He turned the handle of the hurdy-gurdy, a hand-cranked wheel fiddle, which sat on two large wheels. It emitted a gay, rasping sound. The music filled the air, creating a carnival atmosphere that always attracted a small crowd. Pepe, his brown monkey with an intriguing narrow face, wore a plaid skirt, gray vest, and scarlet bonnet. He jumped around on a leash with a tin cup in his hand, approaching the crowd of small children. I made sure to have pennies saved from my ten-cent allowance to drop in the cup. Pepe then nodded at me and looked up at his owner.

The organ grinder reached into his paper bag and handed me a peanut. I, in turn, offered it to Pepe, who gently took it in his paws and popped it into his mouth. Sometimes Mother even dropped a quarter in the cup. The organ grinder tipped his head back laughing and said, "Gracias."

Every Saturday morning Father took his shirts to the Chinese laundry on Montague Street. Dressed in his business suit, he would ceremoniously hoist the white laundry bag over his shoulder. The drawstring dangled down as he set out in his measured stride. I loved to accompany him with Duke, our

English bulldog, but simultaneously shrank with embarrassment at Father's unlikely resemblance to a deliveryman.

Although Bertha the laundress came to do the household laundry every Tuesday, it did not include my Father's shirts. He explained he needed very white shirts with stiff collars and cuffs that only the Chinese laundrymen accomplished. I think he also found something oddly reassuring in his Saturday ritual and depended on it. I imagine he admired the business acumen and hard work of the Chinese laundrymen and sympathized with their lonely existence in a foreign country.

One winter Saturday Father and I strode down to the laundry as usual. The bell jangled as we opened the door and descended the two steps. Mr. Chan, the owner, was dressed in black trousers and a loose-cut cotton jacket. He put down his iron. Showing little facial expression, he made several short bows. In his limited English, he greeted Father with a garbled Chinese version of his name.

Thick steam swirled around the shop, which had its own unique damp laundry smell. Three Chinese male helpers wore similar traditional apparel as they ironed the shirts on long boards. Each spit water through a tube in his mouth to sprinkle the shirts. An experienced worker could iron eighteen shirts an hour.

Father located last week's ticket and placed it on top of his sack of dirty laundry. Mr. Chan quickly ferreted out the package of clean shirts on the shelf. He picked up his

Every Saturday Father took his shirts to be cleaned at the Chinese laundry on Montague Street. Photo courtesy of Ban Seng Hoe

abacus, tallied the bill by rapidly pushing the wooden balls from side to side, and wrote down the amount. An old-fashioned wooden cash drawer was installed underneath the counter. A little bell tinkled as he pulled it open. Apparently, only enough small change for the day was kept there in case of robbery.

It was almost New Year's Day. "You, veddy veddy good customer," Mr. Chan said with a sing-song inflection as he gave us each a little present of lychee nuts, carefully wrapped in red tissue paper, the Chinese symbol of good luck and prosperity. Then most unexpectedly, he offered us a tour of the shop. We recognized this as an honor rarely bestowed upon customers.

He parted the curtained doorway that separated the front and rear parts of the shop. A narrow couch and three army cots, which served as beds, were tucked underneath a shelf stacked with packaged laundry. A drying space was beyond with its tin plates built along the wall, halfway up the ceiling. Overhead a dozen strong iron wires were strung across to hang wet laundry for drying. In the center of this space stood an old-fashioned coal stove, where a coal fire could be built for drying. Farther on were a washing machine, washing sink, lavatory, and steam boiler. A mangle, a large machine with heated rollers for pressing large items such as tablecloths, and a sewing machine sat side by side.

It was evident the shop was a place of work and their home. At closing time, they pulled down the shades to prepare for the night and by placing the ironing boards against the wall. For dinner, one helper cooked rice over a simple two-burner stove.

The 1882 Chinese Exclusion Act had prohibited laborers from entering the United States, although those already here could stay. Their wives and families could not join them, nor could they become naturalized citizens.

Mr. Chan and his employees worked long hours, sometimes from six in the morning until midnight, depending upon the volume of business. On Sunday morning, they would sort the soiled laundry, divide the week's profits, and take the rest of the day off. Mr. Chan rode the subway to Chinatown to buy food and socialize with cousins or clan members. Being Chinese in New York in the '30s meant associating only with other Chinese.

When the laundryman needed more help in his store, he sent a steamship ticket for a young cousin, nephew, or son to join him, as well as paid a 'Head Tax' or otherwise circumventing the 1882 Exclusion Act. Many of these Chinese started laundry businesses with five hundred dollars borrowed from fellow immigrants in the area. Others worked in chop suey restaurants. Neighborhood children naïvely sang a popular ditty with catchy music that referred to these hardworking people in these Chinese laundries: "Chinaman, Chinaman wash my pants; put them in the dryer and watch them dance."

Mr. Chan's family had been simple farmers and laborers in Toyshan County south of Canton (the city now known as Guangzhou). Their dream was to come to "The Golden Mountain," which referred to the California gold rush, when the Chinese reputedly returned with bushels of gold sand.

We thanked Mr. Chan for our New Year's presents and the fascinating tour. Excitement ensued as Father handed each of them a sealed envelope containing crisp new bank bills and a note in celebration of their own Chinese New Year. As we departed, they all held their hands in front of their stomachs and bowed.

Leaving the steam of the shop, we buttoned up against the bitterly cold temperature and walked home without words.

ANTONIO'S HORSE AND CART

One spring morning Mother invited Louise and me to accompany her to run errands around the corner on Montague Street. Little did we suspect the frenzy we would witness in the next few hours.

Youngest sister Louise insisted on riding her new tricycle. I opted to leave my roller skates at home because the Henry Street sidewalks were bumpy and uneven. Montague Street exuded another world, teeming with commercial activity and unfamiliar foreign attributes. I felt impatient to check it all out. Mother walked slowly, waiting for Louise to catch up. Her short legs were pedaling like fury, but progress was snail-paced.

Mother headed to Reeves Market to place her weekend grocery order. As we were about to go into the grocery store, I spied a crowd of people peering down at something on the street in front of the Chinese laundryman's shop. Even Mr. Chan, wearing his black satin trousers and loose top with frog closings, was outside his shop. I saw his pigtail bobbing up and down as he talked.

I rushed over to investigate and ducked between legs to reach the front of the group. There I saw a worn-out horse collapsed. All of his four legs were splayed out. Foam covered his mouth as he wheezed and struggled to breathe. His harness was still attached to the wooden wagon, now broken, which lay on its side. Red tomatoes careened down the street, followed by yellow onions, and heads of lettuce. Carrots with their green tops lay in

The author found sister Louise and her tricycle a distracting nuisance on Montague Street.

heaps while small round potatoes resembled billiard balls rolling in slow motion.

The Italian farmer who owned the horse and wagon gesticulated, waving his hands in the air as he desperately pleaded for help in Italian. No one could understand his words, but it was obvious this was a major loss for him. Apparently, he and the horse had crossed the Brooklyn Bridge from New Jersey early that morning to sell his produce.

"Oh dear," Mother said, "That's Antonio. I always buy onions and lettuce from him on Friday. What a terrible thing. That horse will never make it across the bridge again, and I don't imagine he can afford to buy another."

"The horse looks starved with those ribs pushing through his skin. In fact I think he's almost dead," I observed.

Louise had managed to manipulate her tricycle right behind the horse's rear end and then got her front wheel stuck in a fresh manure patty. She was puzzled what to do because she did not want to step off to push the tricycle, and risk getting her shoes and new leggings all smelly.

"Help! Help!" she yelled, "Someone come immediately. I want to get right out of here now." A handsome man in his gray tweed overcoat and hat rushed to her rescue, yanking the tricycle out of the mushy manure. One of his feet slid into the middle of the patty leaving him with manure covering his shoe and black-striped sock. Louise gaily pedaled off waving her small hand in thanks, her blond curls bouncing on her head, unaware of his remaining dilemma.

People readily came to Louise's rescue, and I begrudgingly attributed it to her blond curls and perky personality. Always concerned about consequences, I wondered what the gentleman would do about his manure-covered shoe: I supposed he would continue to his office, and then clean it and his sock in the washroom, messing up the sink. I pondered whether the bad odor really disappear even after all that.

A couple of policemen sauntered down to assess the horse and discuss the options. The horse weighed between 1,300 and 1,500 pounds; they would need numerous men to lift it. They decided to call for the low-slung vehicle with a hoist and tackle to lift the poor horse onto the flatbed. Then the people and equipment would haul it to a place of disposal. This might take two or three days to coordinate.

After the fuss subsided over the horse and Louise's tricycle, Mother continued her morning errands, picking up a large leg of lamb at the butcher's, then stopping at Spector's on the corner to get Band-Aids, aspirin, toothpaste, and other items for the medicine cabinet. As it was still morning, we did not sit at the counter for an ice cream soda.

We continued to Mr. Pincus' frame shop. A few steps led down to the store so Louise had to leave her tricycle on the sidewalk; she kept glancing up to be sure it was safe. Mr. Pincus excitedly showed us his elephant portfolio of choice Audubon prints; he had just purchased them hoping Mother might be interested. She and I both were holding magnifying glasses to examine the detail of the feathers on the ducks when Louise yelped. She went flying out the door and up the steps to rescue her tricycle from a rough-looking kid who was running down the street with it. She screamed, "Help, help! He's stealing by birthday tricycle!"

Once again, someone came to Louise's rescue—this time one of the policemen who had been standing by the collapsed horse. The young thief shot out of sight and Louise happily pedaled back to the store with the policeman strolling beside her. He chatted with her until Mother finished her business at the frame shop.

On Father's last trip to London, he had purchased a set of prints that Mr. Pincus had framed in proper black Ackerman frames with gold beads around the edges. These were to be hung in his Wall Street office. Father was meticulous about selecting the correct frame to match the period of the print.

Mother carefully lifted the new package of prints and set off again. I followed her up Mr. Pincus' steps where she shook the policeman's hand and thanked him for helping Louise with her almost-stolen tricycle. Louise was pleased when the policeman walked us all down to Ebinger's Bakery.

Ebinger's was a realm unto itself. The bakery was spotless: the outside windows caught the sunlight on bright days, and inside, the cases gleamed. The smells of freshly baked goods wafted out to the sidewalk. Once inside we peered through the glass at the tempting delicacies on the shelves. Mother shopped there once a week for treats and today decided on our favorite pecan coffee ring, and a cake with dark chocolate icing.

A young woman in a white coat carefully took each pastry out of the case, then centered it onto a paper doily and placed it in a white satiny box, which she tied with a string.

By now, Mother was loaded down with packages. I begged to carry the cake, being the elder and vowing how careful I would be not to tip it. Louise was disappointed not to carry any parcels, but she had chosen to come on her tricycle. As I proudly walked out the door, Louise turned her tricycle sharply around and by mistake bumped into me. The cake box flipped out of my hands, landing upside down on the ground. I was mortified.

Mother was annoyed, but understood that it was an accident and resolved it would be sent to the kitchen for the maids. Much to my disappointment, she did not purchase a replacement.

We returned to Remsen Street just in time for Nora's lunch of fried liver and bacon with buttered toast triangles. Bessie listened attentively as we earnestly relayed our misadventures detail by detail. She commented that she was reassured we all returned unharmed after the near catastrophes.

For the next few days after school, I secretly slipped over to check on Antonio's dead horse. The odor turned into a stench as the poor rotting horse carcass lay in the street covered with crawling flies and maggots. People walked by and glanced in its direction and then made a wide arc around it, wishing, of course, that someone would get rid of the appalling mess. On the third day, the horse carcass was gone at last, leaving only a wet outline of body fluids where he had expired.

Via the maids' grapevine, Mother learned Antonio had arrived from Sicily two years before and worked on a farm. He was paid a small wage and had diligently saved his money to buy this old horse. The farmer granted him permission to grow his own produce on a modest plot. He ate part of this bounty and the rest he trundled across the river to sell on Montague Street. We missed him on Fridays after that: Antonio, his horse, his cart, and his vegetables were now gone.

Years later, when I had grown and married, Mother and Father came to visit my husband John and me in our home in Wellesley. Father noticed that John's collection of prints of Trinity College, Cambridge University, was not in the prescribed Ackerman frames, and made quite a fuss about them. Soon after, I dutifully carted all six of them off to the frame shop to be reframed.

CROSSING THE BRIDGE

The maids were Catholic and therefore did not eat meat on Fridays, so Friday was Fish Day. This meant our weekly expedition over Brooklyn Bridge to the Fulton Fish Market. Each morning Long Island and New Jersey vendors brought in fresh produce for the city. They transported it in old farm trucks or by wagons drawn by weary-looking horses.

At the Fulton Market (not then limited to fish and seafood), men noisily hawked their wares. Farther down the strong smell of garbage and manure stung our nostrils—so unlike Montague Street, which was calmer and better mannered. The noise and rough language sounded more like the waterfront area by the docks on Furman Street, where we were forbidden to go alone.

Bushel baskets of vegetables waited for buyers in the sidewalk market: beans, peas, carrots with their frilly green stems, firm red tomatoes arranged in pyramids, all kinds of squash, and small white pearl onions backed by larger yellow ones piled high beside the milder brown Italian ones suitable for salads. Behind all this, braids of garlic hung festively from nails.

Before purchasing oranges, Mother had the man open the crate, then cut an orange so she could taste it. If it was sweet enough, she checked for spoiled ones among the rest. Fruits were only available in season, which added to our anticipation. There was exhilaration when orange persimmons and the large loose-skinned tangerines arrived during the holidays, accompanied by boxes of whole pecans and walnuts.

After Mother made her vegetable purchases and found help to put them in the car, we strode inside the vast warehouse with sawdust on the floor to the meat section. Hooks held entire lambs, huge sides of beef still dripping with blood, rabbits hanging by their feet and chickens with their heads flopping down. This was a more complicated purchase as Mother knew how the meat was to be cooked and would specify which cut she wanted. The butcher struggled getting down the cumbersome side of beef, then positioned it on the slab. In his white apron, now spotted with blood, he took down the longest knife, and ran it across the sharpener before doing the first cut. Then various knives were used to trim the selection and finally shape it into its final form.

Farther down were the fish, the smelliest section, but my favorite. Huge tunas lay on crushed ice next to salmon with their pink meat, then striped bass and cod. These were meticulously arranged in perfectly parallel rows. Mother consulted with the fishmonger dressed in his white coat. If salmon was the choice, she asked, "Which is the freshest, when did it arrive, and is the salmon Alaskan or Norwegian?" At dinner, Father would inquire whether it was Atlantic or Pacific salmon, although I never could taste the difference. Mother and the fishmonger

Crossing the bridge from Brooklyn Heights offered another view of the world, its people, and adventures.

peered in the fishes' eyes, looking for clear ones, as cloudy eyes meant a fish was some days old. The scales were still so shiny they looked as if that had been happily swimming in the ocean the night before. I remember something royal about the large fish with their sleek strong bodies but it puzzled me how the small fins could propel them through water. And the rows of little teeth inside their mouths seemed too tiny.

By now, we had been inside the unheated building for an hour or more. I had become chilly in the dampness and wanted the fishmonger to hurry up and wrap the purchase in heavy white paper so we could continue. Besides, down the aisle was a counter with nut and raisin bars three-inches long, which I hoped Mother might purchase for my treat.

The last purchase was fresh flowers. The vendor carts were along the curb outside the market. Mother would slowly walk by, looking for certain varieties or colors, while checking which flowers were the freshest that week. Buying flowers always had a different feeling to it, a bit gayer and more frivolous; flowers were a luxury and not as serious as the food purchases.

When we got home, Nora would scrutinize all the food, clucking her tongue and commenting on the quality and freshness. Louise and I often went to the basement and sat at the long kitchen table to help Nora and Bessie. Time in the kitchen meant catching up on neighborhood gossip, usually relayed by the Irish policemen who had married Bessie and Nora's nieces. Listening intrigued us because the conversation differed so from the sedate exchanges Mother had with friends.

Later, the prepared meals came up to the pantry on the dumbwaiter and Bessie brought them to the dinner table where Father would either praise them, or not. But the flowers were just between Bessie and Mother. When Mother handed them to her, Bessie would clap her hands, delighted with whatever they were. She accepted them as if they were her own special present.

At four o'clock, Bessie served us tea and cookies, she and Nora had already enjoyed theirs in the kitchen. Then everything accelerated into full gear for dinner. The tall pot was filled with water to boil potatoes for the fish, and then the salmon was carefully arranged in a net and put in a pan for poaching on top of the black iron stove. This would be served with a white sauce with diced eggs in it. Mother always had peas with salmon as well as another vegetable, and of course, fresh rolls. Nora would often have baked a pie that morning which would be served with cheese. "A pie without cheese is like a kiss without a squeeze," Mother would remind us when the two pie plates were placed before her. She carefully sliced pieces with the silver pie server, placing each on a dessert plate, which Bessie then served to us. Occasionally whipped cream or ice cream would be in a glass bowl; we would help ourselves and there might even be pecan pieces to sprinkle on top.

Two hours later, it was the end of another delicious meal. This particular evening I counted fifteen people around the table and marveled at how quickly everything had been eaten. I recalled the daylong adventures from the morning at the Fulton Fish Market, to the kitchen, the evening meal, and now, dinner's end: we were drowsy and content.

Gypsies under the Brooklyn Bridge

"Look at those braids and ribbons in their hair! And those long skirts…They've got bracelets up their arms…wish I could have some like that. Something is sparkling in the sunlight. It must be their necklaces of gold coins," I said to my younger sister Louise.

The gypsies were under the Brooklyn Bridge. Father had seen them that morning as he walked to Wall Street. Now Mother was driving to the Fulton Fish Market and she slowed down as we drove onto the Brooklyn Bridge, pointing out the gypsies. Louise and I craned our necks and peered out the window to see what was going on below. We thought we saw some tents as well as a couple of wagons and horses. Smoke curled up from a portable coal stove where the small community of gypsies appeared to be cooking.

The men were dressed in baggy black trousers, shirts, and vests; some wore high boots and broad felt hats. Their hammers were pounding away on an anvil. Mother was equally curious but didn't dare take her attention away from the traffic jam on the bridge.

For some time we had heard rumors about the gypsies under the bridge. Someone had spotted them on Fulton Street by Borough Hall and two gypsies had set up fortune-telling tables in a nearby storefront. Louise and I were disappointed that they never wandered as far as Montague Street or our neighborhood.

Of course, I was dying to sneak down and have my fortune read, but I knew how Mother and Father would react to such an adventure: that area was out-of-bounds. Anyway, I didn't have the nerve to go alone nor did I want to get any friends in trouble. The tales of gypsies kidnapping children scared me.

Louise and I couldn't wait to get home and tell Bessie and Nora. They could gather additional information for us from the Irish policemen who knew about everything going on in the vicinity.

The next day at Packer, I went to the library to take out two books on gypsies so that I could learn more about their foreign customs. After finishing those, I went to the public library on Montague Street and found a couple of more about gypsies in the United States. I soon became immersed in their culture and fantasized I was one of them.

I learned that the gypsies were nomads and originated in northern India. They called themselves Romas or Romanies and had their own language. They had wandered up through Bulgaria, Serbia, and Romania, and then spread into Russia, and eastern and western Europe. They often spoke five or six languages. In Europe, gypsies would wanderer from country to country and were not welcome anywhere. They traveled in caravans, camping in towns with their parade of horses, painted wagons, and tents. They often stole chickens and rarely ingratiated themselves or contributed to the community. Some groups repaired pots and pans, or mended bridles and harnesses.

Many English gypsies were deported in colonial days, arriving here in the late 1800s. They needed a country that was not too settled so they could camp where they pleased. But they did not want their new "home" too thinly inhabited or too poor because they depended on the prosperity of others.

Of course, I shared this information with my best friends, lending them the books. We decided to form a Gypsy Club that was open only by invitation. We would tell each other stories. One day I noticed an upperclassman at chapel in a long swirly skirt; her dark hair was braided with ribbons and she was wearing six bracelets on her arm. As we sang the last hymn, I kept standing on tiptoe to further scrutinize her strange outfit.

She claimed to have gypsy blood that had been kept a dark secret in her family. The teachers seemed uncomfortable with her unusual dress, but she was an excellent student and except for certain eccentricities, did not cause trouble. No one quite knew whether to believe her because she was always rather theatrical and loved to exaggerate. Her parents were Lebanese, so her olive skin and black eyes certainly allowed her to look the part.

Our Gypsy Club swelled to six members and we swore to treat our meetings with the greatest of secrecy. We were fascinated that gypsies could barely read or write and that none of the children went to school.

"Think of the women supporting the family by fortune-telling, and making hundreds of dollars a year for their fathers or husbands," my friend Jane commented. "I wouldn't want to be sold as a bride at fourteen or fifteen years old and wander around for the rest of my life with my husband's family," our friend Cynthia said. The payment was to compensate the bride's family of origin for the loss of a breadwinner. Sue, a third Gypsy Club member, piped up, "And the men trade horses, which is so different from what our fathers do."

The more we learned the more exotic and mysterious their lives seemed. But I questioned how clever a fortune-teller I would be…reading palms, looking for "heart lines," and "mounts of Saturn." Oh, to rid ourselves of stuffy rules and have all that freedom! Our restrained existence suddenly seemed so confined. And those hideous curses they put on people—then taking money and doing the switch and bait trick. "How awful to live on the fringe of society and not belong anywhere or be accepted by anyone," I pondered.

Our gypsy experience was becoming so intense I had a nightmare where I had been kidnapped by a gypsy troupe that had taken off across the country in their wagons. I was a hostage. What a relief it was when daylight arrived and I woke up in my own bedroom on the third floor of 82 Remsen Street.

One day I found a palmistry card in my older brother's desk and borrowed it for our club meeting. We read each other's palms with it and made up wild things about what we saw in one another's future. We solemnly promised not to fool around with curses. It was about this time we began to spook ourselves, and eventually we tired of the play.

Meanwhile, Mother became suspicious of the hushed phone calls and frequent meetings at friends' houses. I didn't want to meet at our house because I suspected she might disapprove of the club. Then I began wearing bright ribbons in my hair, as did the other club members, and I asked Mother for a long skirt, which she refused to buy for me. I don't even remember if stores sold them at that time.

Finally, Nora gave us the long-awaited report from Patrick, the Irish policeman who married Bebe: Yes, the gypsies were camped under the Brooklyn Bridge, and this particular group had arrived from Brazil via Cuba. The police were keeping an eye on them but there was nothing illegal about their being there. Reports of stolen wallets and pocketbooks increased, but the thieves could never be traced.

However, one Sunday night there was a noisy ruckus among them and knives were drawn. We learned later that a gypsy father had betrothed his fourteen-year-old daughter to the groom's family for two thousand dollars. As was the custom, the money was to be paid in gold coins, and this payment was five hundred dollars short. The groom's father refused to pay the rest, saying he heard rumors the girl was not a virgin. A terrible brawl broke out between both families. The police arrived and determined the dispute should be settled in court. But the gypsies knew they would be in trouble; the girl was underage by law. Somehow, a group of them diverted the police while the rest pulled down their tents, loaded the wagons, headed over the bridge, and disappeared. As unlikely as it sounds, the police were unable to find them.

Another group of gypsies lived in buildings between Fifth and Ninth Streets on the New York's East Side; Patrick thought they might have taken in "our" band. Yet the mystery remained. What had happened to the horses and wagons? Vanishing was a skill that gypsies worldwide seemed to have perfected.

This report of violence confirmed the club's worst fears and severely diminished the allure of gypsy life. Although we never forgot the gypsies' short stay near our neighborhood, or the solidarity of community they inadvertently taught us, the yellow forsythia were blooming in the front yards and warmer breezes wafted off the East River. Spring was coming right along with the Good Humor man and his familiar tinkling bell. Our own Gypsy Club quietly disbanded as we happily dragged out our roller skates.

CHAPTER 4

Pastimes

A Magical Children's Garden

Brooklyn Heights boasted an abundance of trees but no parks or grassy areas, so Miss White's garden became a botanical sanctuary for young children. A tall black wrought-iron fence surrounded the garden and encompassed the entire block. Miss White lived in a large brownstone across the street and loved children, although she had none of her own. From her second floor window, she took pleasure in watching the activity of the youngsters in her garden.

Louise and I looked forward to our outings with Mother to Miss White's garden. But you needed the key. Access into the xs out keys. Miss White would ask the local pediatrician for the names of young mothers with preschoolers who might be interested. The criteria for selection were somewhat mysterious. If a mother's name was given to Miss White for consideration, she would telephone to announce that her secretary would drop in during the next week to meet mother and child. This visit might be during the early dinner hours when households were inclined to be chaotic. It was said that your housekeeping abilities were noted, as these reflected upon how you conducted your life as well.

A week or so later the secretary would personally deliver an envelope with a short note on engraved stationery saying either it was not possible to grant you access to the garden or a formal note of welcome, which included detailed protocols and a gleaming

Alice and Louise in the garden in their summer hats.

new key. Of course, no dogs or pets were allowed and the last family to leave the garden was to place the net on the sand piles to protect them against the roving pussycats. Everyone took these rules seriously as an unnerving tale circulated about a little boy whom Miss White saw peeing in the bushes. She requested that the key be returned immediately.

Our key marked "Miss White's Garden" on the attached white cardboard circle was kept in the middle drawer of the leather-topped desk that stood against the wall of the entryway. It lay there with other important keys, such as ones to the wine cellar and the Cadillac and Chevy that were kept in the back garage. Louise and I were not allowed to open that drawer or touch the keys. However, I often secretly pulled it open to be sure the key was safely there. I could not read the labels at that time, but I knew it was the shiny key.

From 82 Remsen Street it was a pleasant stroll to Miss White's garden. Louise and I walked on either side of Mother, holding her hand and swinging our little pails with shovels in our free hands. As we approached the garden, we peered through the wrought-iron fence to see if any friends were there. Mother then took the key out of her pocket, unlocked the gate, shut and latched it carefully behind us after we entered.

The garden was an enchanted space. One path led to the right and another to the left with an area of manicured grass. There were lovely trees, shrubbery, and seasonal flowers. In the back were two sand piles, a larger one for the older children, and a sunken one for the smaller ones—a rarity in the city. We usually found a few children we knew who made room for us in the sand pile area while Mother chatted to friends on a nearby bench, leaving us to enjoy ourselves. We were enclosed in our private world of play and laughter unaware of the traffic on the streets as the outside world conducted its business.

Then, promptly at 11:45 a.m., it was time to pack up and leave as lunch would await us at home and naps would then follow. As an extra treat, Mother would sometimes read a chapter from *The Secret Garden,* which resonated in my young mind from the recent visit.

By the time I was in kindergarten, we did not go to Miss White's garden, and it receded as part of my early childhood routine. However, I often roller-skated or walked by to observe the garden through the iron fence and reassure myself that all was well....

Miss White died in the late 1940s and the magical garden was sold. The fence was rapidly knocked down. Trees were brutally uprooted, dangling in the air as they were dropped into trucks to be carted off to the dump. Bulldozers clamored down the street. Steel-jawed shovels gobbled up the brick walks, grass, and shrubbery, as well as our beloved sand piles. The frightening din and clashing of machinery ripped the garden apart. There was increasing dust and noise as even larger equipment rattled down to decimate the area. They dug and dug deep into the ground to bedrock, without consideration of the garden's soul or the history of childhood memories or the beauty they were destroying. Satisfied, they poured concrete, put in footings and pillars, and started building two monstrous apartment houses that loomed above all the brownstones on the street. Rows and rows of uninteresting windows dominated and seemed to mock the area.

They were finished and two enormous apartment houses at 57 Montague Street and 2 Pierrepont Street stood in the place of the garden. Breezes and sunshine were blocked out and the soft rain no longer nurtured grass and shrubbery. The birds and butterflies as well as the children that once graced the garden would have to go elsewhere. I stopped walking by, finding it too painful to see the ugliness that thrust itself above our once magical place.

Later, as I grew older and became aware of cliques in school, I wondered how exclusionary it must have felt for young mothers and their children not to be granted the privilege of the key.

Eventually, a sizable playground with swings, a jungle gym, and slides was built across Pierrepont Place leading onto the promenade. Now all young mothers could take their children in strollers or on tricycles for outings. Couples could walk, and even much older people could be pushed in wheelchairs or could sit on the benches to chat or watch the boats ply the East River. I applauded the playground's vastness and availability to a spectrum of people and all ages.

Roller Skates and Dy-Dee Dolls

One Christmas a shoe box-sized package sat under our tree wrapped in paper with holly decorations. When my younger sister Louise and I crept down that early morning to open our stockings, I picked up this mysterious package with my name on it and tried to rattle it. It was heavy for a pair of shoes.

Finally, when the rest of the family assembled to open presents after breakfast, I tore the wrappings off the hefty box to reveal a brand new pair of roller skates with a shiny key.

I threaded the key through some string and immediately tied it around my neck so I wouldn't lose it. The skates fit perfectly over my brown oxford lace-up shoes. I had to wait impatiently through the Christmas celebration with its festive dinner and the opening of presents before I could try them out.

The weather was moderate for Christmas day and I sat on our stoop thrusting my shoes in the clamps and buckling the leather strap across my instep on these handsome unscratched roller skates. I turned the key and tightened the skates to adjust the tension. Standing up unsteadily, I put one foot gingerly in front of the other. I stumbled clumsily to the end of Remsen Street, cautiously pushing each foot slightly ahead. After a few times back and forth I began to feel steadier and took off with more confidence.

Now I was ready for an audience. I called Louise, who followed me on her tricycle and gave me encouragement. The next day I summoned my friends, Jean McKee and Patty Foote, who had also received skates for Christmas. We met to accompany each other up and down the middle of Remsen Street, which had no traffic that day. Oh, the independence!

What a sense of accomplishment and freedom we all felt that week as we investigated Montague Street and Monroe Place, where we glided along the newest and smoothest sidewalks. We raced to the foot of Remsen Street to check out the cargo ships below and laughed with glee at the chinckety-chinckety sound our skates made as we rolled over the cracks. We delighted in the speed with which we could cover the neighborhood, and the joy of traveling so rapidly. Two wheelers were considered dangerous with the traffic, so roller skates became our transportation option.

I preferred these outdoor activities, and so dolls never held my interest, with one exception: I craved the Dy-Dee Doll at A&S. She was out of my budget at $4.75; there seemed no way I could save enough of my 15-cent allowance to pay for her. Nonetheless, I realized even then that my weekly allotment was generous for the time; the maids earned $20 a week and worked long hours.

Dy-Dee Doll was made of rubber, wore a bonnet, and was dressed in a pink flannel dress trimmed with a row of rickrack around the collar. She was displayed in her very own box with clasps that shut, and a handle on the outside. Surrounding her were three new diapers with safety pins and a little bottle with a nipple. You could fill the bottle with water and feed her. She immediately wet her diapers, which then needed to be changed. The thought of owning this doll just thrilled me. I longed to wash the diapers with soapsuds in the sink and hang them on the bathroom towel rack to dry.

Someone reported to me that in Montreal at Simpson's department store the Dy-Dee dolls were in bassinets in a nursery with white uniformed nurses attending them, rocking the dolls in their arms, feeding them their bottles, and changing their diapers.

For weeks, I talked about this doll, and dragged Mother to A&S so she could admire her with me. Mother thought it a silly idea as she had changed diapers for her six children and did not understand my fascination with this doll. November, my birthday month, passed…no Dy-Dee Doll. Christmas came and there was still no Dy-Dee Doll waiting for me under the tree. All hope seemed gone.

Then one warm April day when the forsythia bushes were in bloom all over the Heights, Mother seemed especially elated. She announced we were going on a surprise errand. I sensed something unusual and hustled to put on my coat as off we went hand in hand to A&S.

She told the saleswoman, "I want to purchase a Dy-Dee Doll for my wonderful young daughter who has been so helpful and patient." I stood there and almost cried with surprise and excitement. I had never heard such praise and I didn't realize I had done anything special to earn this reward. However, my sister Louise had been sick recently, and although I didn't do anything particular or unusual, I cared visibly and I would have been devastated if anything serious had happened to Louise.

Mother handed the sales lady a five-dollar bill, counted the change, and put it in her purse. The salesperson asked if I would like Dy-Dee in a bag or preferred to carry her out by the handle on the case. Of course, I wanted to hold the handle so everyone we passed could see what a desirable present I had. I walked and skipped, and couldn't stop talking the whole way home. Mother said, "I'm sorry you had to wait so long; I guess I didn't realize how much you wanted her." I discussed changing her name with Mother but decided Dy-Dee Doll suited her just perfectly.

The minute I got home, I raced to the phone to call Patty Foote and tell her my unbelievable news. That week every friend came to watch me feed my Dy-Dee Doll and change her diapers. I wouldn't let anyone else hold her or feed her. Three diapers were hardly enough with all the drinking she did, so our nursemaid Bebe made me more diapers out of some white material from the rag bag. She cut them with pinking shears so they looked rather fancy. Our bathroom towel racks were filled with tiny, newly washed diapers. I felt it proper Dy-Dee spend her nights in her own little bed covered with a blanket, which I placed on the floor beside mine. If she woke up during the night, I could attend to her.

This routine went on all spring and Dy-Dee traveled with us to Maine that summer. By then I was tiring of her time-consuming routine so I put her back in her original box and deposited it in the corner closet. My attention turned to swimming, canoeing, and our other out-doors activities.

Another item I craved was a Popeye-the-Sailor-Man watch. Louise had received her Mickey Mouse watch that Christmas and she was getting so many compliments that I wanted a Popeye one. These cartoon characters were everywhere, from the comic strips to the movie shorts. I loved Popeye with his bulging biceps and taste for spinach to keep him fit. There was even a song about him. Olive Oyl, his girlfriend, was constantly by his side.

The watch cost $3.98 and was therefore another yearning beyond my means. I asked Mother if I could earn the money by organizing all the holiday wrapping paper and ribbons, as well as two drawers in the file cabinet filled with string. Each December after wrapping our family's Christmas presents the second floor front room became an unholy mess.

Mother agreed to the proposal and organizing all of the wrapping and trim excited me. I took each tube, tightened the paper around it, and secured it with a rubber band. I folded the tissue paper in piles according to color and placed them in a box.

I even ironed the used satin ribbons and twirled them onto a cardboard roll.

I located fresh containers for the paper clips and rubber bands, stacked note pads together in cubbyholes in the desk and even lined up the erasers in neat rows. I untangled the mess in the string drawer. After this was finished, Mother inspected the orderliness and seemed impressed with my abilities. She promised a trip to A&S that very Saturday to purchase the Popeye watch.

We walked to the store and I looked at all the cartoon watches in the glass case. I was tempted by Goofy and Donald Duck but finally returned to Popeye as my favorite.

After all, I loved spinach as much as he did. It empowered him to defeat his foes. And he sucked it right out of the can with his pipe, and then strutted around flexing his muscles and singing Popeye-the-Sailor-Man in his gravelly voice. His speech was appalling and never would have been permitted at home: "Strong to the finich, I eats my spinach," or, "I yam what I yam an' tha's all that I yam; I'm-Popeye-the-Sailor-Man!"

I suppose I connected him with the burly longshoremen on those big ships docked at the foot of Remsen Street; Popeye always tried to do the right thing and defend the underdog.

I wound the watch each morning and wore it so constantly the straps had to be replaced twice. Two years later, I dropped it on our bathroom floor, the spring broke, and time stood still for Popeye.

FALSE ALARM

One year when summer had long retreated and we had returned to Remsen Street and back to school, our regular routines were turned upside down by a mysterious illness and startling diagnosis.

Louise, older brother Bob, and I had persistent coughs for two weeks that sounded different from the usual one that accompanies colds. I did not remember feeling ill; it was more of a nuisance.

Dr. Given, our kind and competent pediatrician, was away so Mother called Dr. Z., who was available, but in whom she had little faith. He arrived with his black bag, opened it, and took out his stethoscope to listen to our breathing.

A troubled look shadowed his face as he shook his head. He reached into his bag and put a patch on the upper part of our arms, called a "patch test." This was to remain on overnight. The next day he returned to take it off and read it.

According to him, we all tested positive for tuberculosis (TB). We were immediately driven to Long Island College Hospital for lung x-rays. A young radiologist jauntily arrived in his white coat to read the x-rays; he pronounced that all of us had full-blown cases of TB. No children at either our girls' school, Packer, or the boys' school, Poly Prep, had reported having TB, although some cases had been seen in the surrounding area.

Recovery rules were strict: bed rest for many months with only trips to the bathroom and a quick sponge bath every evening. This bed rest would enable our lungs to heal. All meals were to be brought up on trays and eaten in bed.

It seemed strange to me that one day I was feeling fine and then suddenly, I was considered seriously ill. I knew what sick felt like and this was certainly not it.

Within twenty-four hours, Mother had arranged everything to carry us through this unexpected turn of events. Nurse Svobodka, from Czechoslovakia, was hired to tend to our needs.

She had cared for Grandfather Hooker during his final illness and Mother found her very competent. She was a tall, humorless, no-nonsense woman with her dark hair pulled back tightly in a bun. She appeared each morning in a stiffly starched white uniform and rarely smiled.

Nurse Svobodka saw to it that we drank enough liquids. She took our temperature several times a day, which she painstakingly recorded in a black notebook. Mid-afternoon she brought up three large, rich, frothy eggnogs on a tray.

Mother told us she had been trained from the "old school"—whatever that meant. I certainly was not impressed, except for her sensible lace-up shoes, which were very white with fresh polish applied each night.

Lessons to ensure we did not get behind in our class work were brought daily by two teachers: one from Packer and one from Poly

Following weeks of prolonged and unnecessary bed rest, the author enjoyed her return to school, friends, and childhood play.

Prep. They explained the assignments. But the novelty of staying home from school and having meal trays brought up soon faded. Life became monotonous as the days and weeks dragged on.

No friends were allowed to visit because we were contagious. Bob was on the third floor, Louise and I in the bedroom we shared on the second floor, so we had virtually no contact with him. The one telephone was in the phone closet on the first floor, with no way for us to reach it. The dome-shaped radio in its big wooden brown case stood stayed in the downstairs living room. Television did not exist.

Louise and I played endless card games such as Pounce and gin rummy. Monopoly occupied a fair portion of our days, interspersed with Parcheesi and checkers.

"When can we go back to school? We have been in bed for two months now! It is so boring. I know I'm not sick and I miss all my friends," I pleaded with Dr. Z.

Nurse Svobodka was everywhere; we were convinced she had eyes in the back of her head. This left little chance for mischief, as young people who bent the rules did not amuse her. In fact, I don't think she even liked children.

Louise and I indulged in a favorite circus game in the few times Nurse Svobodka was out of sight. I lay on my back and Louise, tummy down, poised herself on my outstretched feet in a balancing act.

We fancied an audience in bleachers roaring with applause as I pushed Louise up and down and she waved and nodded to them. We fantasized we were acrobats in fancy, bright, tight-fitting costumes with black fishnet tights, nothing to do with real life. We laughed and laughed, until we heard Nurse Svobodka's footsteps. Louise would jump back into her bed, pull up the covers and we shut our eyes to pretend we were napping, so she wouldn't give us yet another lecture.

Mother finally became uneasy about our four-and-a-half month course of treatment, so Father summoned his brother, Uncle Douglas Davidson, who was a physician in Delaware. He immediately drove up in his black Cadillac. He examined each of us, listening to our lungs. Then he conferred with the doctors at Long Island College Hospital and scrutinized the x-rays himself. He was puzzled to find them clear with no signs of TB.

It turned out the young radiologist had made a mistake in reading them and no one had questioned his diagnosis. To our surprise, Dr. Z. assured everyone that he had never agreed with the diagnosis but had stood by the radiologist. Everyone knew three Davidson children had been in bed those months, so the diagnosis reversal turned into a bit of a scandal.

The next day we were proclaimed well and ecstatically returned to school. We were tired those first days but our energy returned quickly; however, there was one unfortunate consequence of months spent in bed. I tended to be pudgy and gained over fifteen pounds from the frothy milkshakes and inactivity; I had to be careful about my weight for the rest of my life.

SNOWBANKS AND SLEDDING

Louise and I heard the rumble of the snowplow outside and rushed to draw the curtains. There lay a glorious foot of pristine snow piled up on the side of the street and beckoning to us. We relished these heavy winter snowfalls as it meant hours of romping in the snow. The snow banks on Remsen Street could be impressively high: five or six feet after a series of snowfalls.

Bebe helped us pull on our Best & Co. navy blue snowsuits made of rough scratchy wool, first the baggy pants with elastic at the ankles, then a jacket with a zipper and hood, and finally heavy rubber galoshes with four clasps that Bebe helped us fasten. We tucked the snow pants inside the top to prevent the snow from filling our boots.

Louise and I were especially proud of our red sailor-type hats, scarves, and mittens; we had knit them in Maine that summer under the patient tutelage of Grandmother Hiles and Auntie Pasco. Bebe helped us clip the mittens to our jacket sleeves so we would not be like the three little kittens that lost their mittens.

As we opened the front door, we blinked in the bright sunshine. We could hear neighborhood children laughing and calling back and forth to each other. They summoned us to join in the merriment. We climbed to the top of the mounds by kicking footholds in the snow, then sat on our fannies and shoved off to glide down.

Rarely would a car creep down before the street had been plowed, but still, Bebe reminded us to be cautious. Some years earlier my older sister Kitty was out on a similar day and slid into the back wheel of an oncoming car. The driver was unaware of what happened and just continued down to Hicks Street. Kitty's face had been cut and she injured her eye. Fortunately, Dr. Freeman Love happened to lumber by just then in his chauffeur-driven car. Seeing blood in the snow, he got out, scooped Kitty up, and took her to the Long Island College Hospital where they were able to stitch her up and save her eye.

Of course, every winter we built impressive snowmen, mainly team efforts with nearby friends. We took turns building them in front of a different house each time. Nora was generous about giving us a carrot for the nose and Bebe diligently searched the sewing box for big black coat buttons for the eyes. These creations were a source of pride for us all and admired by the parents on the street.

By noon, we were hungry and ready to return home for lunch. Our wool suits were so covered with snow that Bebe took us in through the basement. Melted snow had made our snowsuits heavy and soggy it was decidedly more arduous to pull the wet clothing off than it had been to put it on. Bebe tapped ice off the clasps on our galoshes, unhooked them, and pulled them from our outstretched legs. A bunch of snow inevitably plopped out on the floor. We shook snow off our hats and mittens, placed them on the radiator to dry, and vigorously rubbed our hands together. We giggled at each other's rosy cheeks and runny noses. Nora's hot soup, followed by liver with toast squares and sausage, tasted mighty good, especially swirled down with a glass of milk.

After another week of snowfalls, it seemed an ideal day to sled down the hill under Penny Bridge, which ended at the waterfront. Bebe never seemed keen about this prospect, perhaps foreseeing some danger in the steepness.

On this day, we pleaded, "But Bebe, we haven't even had our sleds out yet and it's such a perfect day." Mother gave her permission and Bebe agreed to take us.

After tugging on snowsuits, Louise and I thumped across the garden in our galoshes to the carriage house and fetched our Flexible Flyer sleds.

They had wooden slat tops and a wooden steering mechanism attached to a loop of hemp cord. Lying on our stomachs, we could pull the string to direct the sled left or right.

We pulled the sleds to the downstairs workshop where we took the small can of oil with a spout to apply a squirt to the steering. The runners were of black steel.

Louise and I carried our sleds down Remsen to Montague Street with Bebe. Mother accompanied us because she planned to leave a note for someone at One Pierrepont Street.

As I positioned my sled at the top of the hill, I promised Bebe I would not go all the

Louise is pictured playing in the snow outside Packer Collegiate Institute. Brooklyn Heights was filled with opportunity for outdoor winter adventures.

way to the bottom but instead run up into the snow bank halfway down. I took off confidently but the surface was unexpectedly slick and I was soon whizzing out of control. I couldn't turn into the snow bank and felt a mounting panic as the sled gathered momentum. Not only couldn't I stop, I couldn't even veer left or right.

Suddenly, at the very bottom of the hill, I careened into a railroad car parked on the tracks and then I blacked out. Meanwhile Bebe saw Mother returning from her errand

and vigorously waved her arms. Both women tore down the hill, half running, half sliding, to rescue me. Together they pulled the sled up the steep incline as I lay on it, unconscious but breathing. Louise followed behind doing her best to help; she ended up performing the vital task of toting Mother's handbag. They hurried home and carried me upstairs to bed.

The next thing I remember seeing was Dr. Given, with his stethoscope hanging around his neck, examining me. He cleaned my face with a damp washcloth and found only minor scratches. However, a bump on my lower thigh swelled and swelled from broken blood vessels and later became a full-blown hematoma.

Louise tried to comfort and entertain me with her picture books and hovered by my side. The next afternoon she went down to the kitchen to ask Nora for two cups of hot chocolate and newly baked cookies so we could have tea together. Louise carefully brought this up on a tray all by herself. After we finished she put her favorite doll in the crook of my arm and I felt greatly soothed.

My recovery turned into a rare moment between sisters when Louise entreated, "Ali, if you just get well I'll promise never to argue with you again." In a weak voice, I replied, "And I'll stop bossing you around."

SMOOTH SKATING

"Bebe, please, please take us skating this afternoon. The sun is out, the rink is frozen, and I haven't even tried out my new ice skates."

Mother had bought me a grown-up pair of ice skates with laces for my birthday because after a year's practice on shiny double-runners, I was finally able to maneuver the rink without falling.

Importantly, I took my new white leather figure skates out of the big box to demonstrate them to my little sister Louise. I paraded around the living room Oriental rug, and was even able to stand on the rounded saw-toothed tips called toe rakes. They comfortably dug into the plush carpet leaving a little track in the pile, as I explained that this is how you started a twirl. Fortunately, Mother did not happen by at that moment.

Louise and I rushed through lunch, tugged on our woolen snowsuits, and slung our skates over our shoulders like big girls. Bebe followed with a thermos of hot chocolate and two cookies for each of us. We hastened up to the corner of Hicks Street where the empty lot had been magically turned into an ice rink for the neighborhood children.

At noon, someone had brushed and scraped the ice, then flooded it with the hose to leave the ice surface even and glassy. Children were just beginning to get on the ice and Louise and I sat down on a bench. I took off my galoshes, put my feet in the skates, and laced them up. Bebe helped Louise put the double runners over her boots and strapped them on.

Little Louise took off immediately with no trouble, but I found myself wobbling on my new skates as I pushed ahead on the ice. I started out cautiously as this was not as smooth skating as I had envisioned. Jeannie McKee confidently skated over to encourage me and said this was the third time she had been out on her brand-new skates. She looked like an expert as she put one foot in front of the other and slid ahead. Her older sister Betty and cousin Connie Latson, who seemed so competent in everything, were tentatively clutching each other trying to get their balance.

In later years, there were other neighborhood rinks. Two of the tennis courts on the corner of Henry and Remsen Streets were regularly flooded and turned into a skating rink, which afforded considerably more space for skaters. The owner was meticulous about keeping the ice in good shape and was there on skates at all times to supervise. This rink was busier than our little one had been. Some of the skaters were accomplished and they would show off their fancy turns or jumps while the rest of us melted over to the sidelines to watch.

Many times a clutch of older girls would be in the center gossiping about the boys. I must say I liked the games of tag with the boys, when we touched or bumped into each other–awkward hints at the mysteries of adolescence. As dusk crept in, it seemed to cast a mysterious glow and hovering suggestion of romance.

The older boys from Poly Prep who fancied themselves would-be hockey players with their long-bladed skates could be pests. They circled round the rink, bodies bent close to the ice, arms pumping up and down as if racing for the puck. A meany might even try to trip you up and laugh as he whizzed by leaving you trying to regain your balance. It was doubly annoying if a boy, nicely mannered at Miss Hepburn's Dancing School, had a crush on you and thought of this as a flirtatious gesture.

Some children went regularly to the Ice Palace for lessons and became quite proficient. I accompanied friends a few times. A large commercial rink drew children and adults from a wide area. I felt uneasy, as everyone seemed to skate round and round so fast, and occasionally, someone knocked into you, but he or she never offered an apology. I never liked the heavy damp air or the echoing noise from the music, or the clanking as children stomped on and off the ice. It seemed unattractive and artificial.

At the Henry Street rink, a one-time occurrence generated great interest. A Heights' family had houseguests from Boston who had been competition skaters and they offered to give a demonstration on a designated Saturday at 11 a.m. The children and many parents arrived early and excitedly squeezed together on the benches.

A phonograph and dance records had been assembled. The husband and wife were tall and handsome, she with blond hair in a braid and dressed in a red flippy short skirt over black tights, and he in black trousers, white shirt, red bow tie with a short red jacket.

The music started and each came from opposite ends of the rink to meet in the middle. He bowed formally from the waist, took her in skating position and off they went full speed gaining momentum as they circled the rink doing crossovers. Next, they did a bunny hop, followed by spread eagles, sit spins, back spins, and loop jumps. Then the salchow and a waltz jump, all seemingly done without effort.

I was mesmerized by their rhythm and style. Suddenly they pulled slightly apart and both began to spin faster and faster, her pigtail flying in the air, then slower and slower until they came to a complete stop. We stood up and clapped as if we were in a stadium.

There was a pause while someone turned over the record and fiddled with the player to get it going again. Waltz music started as he held her firmly in dance position while he skated forward and she backward.

They bent and swayed in perfect unison incorporating many of the earlier steps they had demonstrated. Everyone's attention was riveted on this lovely scene before us and as the music concluded we all stood up begging for more. The skaters graciously thanked us and left the ice. We were so inspired by their dazzling performance that we all skated far above our usual level that afternoon.

That small vacant lot on Hicks Street with its diminutive ice rink always remained my childhood favorite. During a cold winter, we could skate from November until March with the winter sun or evening streetlights shining down. Trees, streetlights, and handsome brownstone houses surrounded this diminutive neighborhood ice rink on a small vacant lot on Hicks Street. Mr. Butler, the mounted policeman, sometimes meandered by on his horse Gallop, waved, and called us by name. No country setting has ever offered a more enchanting childhood of winter play than did Brooklyn Heights with its city snowbanks, ice rinks, and neighborhood charmed with spirit and soul.

Chapter 5

Shenanigans

Hide-and-Seek Hobgoblins

Louise and I liked to keep track of everything going on in the household. We were especially drawn to areas that were off-limit, such as the basement where most the washing and cooking took place. It was often worth the occasional quick check of the sub-cellar and the carriage house too.

Nora intrigued me, bustling about the kitchen tending her pots, giving one a quick stir with a long wooden spoon, sliding her mitt on to check the contents of the oven, and hustling to the icebox for more butter or cream to add to the sauce. When she had extra time, she might make a double batch of fragrant chocolate chip cookies, the surfaces bumpy with nuts and chocolate bits. Her round figure bent over to lift out the cookie sheet, and then straightened up to place it carefully on the counter, deftly loosening each delicacy with a spatula. When cool, these were stacked in a tall glass cookie jar, the heavy lid was secured, and the sealed goodies were sent by dumbwaiter to Bessie in the pantry. It was understood we were allowed one or two after school with a glass of milk but we were not to be piggy and take more. There was also an unspoken rule that no one was to pluck the raisins or nuts off the top of the Ebinger's coffee cake. But I often did that very thing, carefully, hoping I could smooth over the little holes with the white sugar frosting. Unfortunately, Bessie was quick to catch such tampering.

The laundry room was across the hall from the basement kitchen and was lively on Mondays when the laundress arrived. The washing machine fairly jumped about on its legs as clothes churned around. Meanwhile table linens soaked in the adjacent gray soapstone sinks. In the afternoons, damp smells wafted about as she ironed the sprinkled items and neatly piled them to carry upstairs. The clean, sharp odor of ironed clothes swirled with the heavy humidity that spread throughout the basement casting a haze.

By contrast, on Thursday afternoon, the maids' time off, the empty basement became transformed into an eerie place, as if the whole area was stilled. The endless dark corridor stretched the entire length of the house from the garden to the front. Outside, three steps down from the garden led to the basement. I was always nervous that some stranger might have sneaked inside and would suddenly jump out at me.

I rarely answered the downstairs doorbell, even though I could check who it was through the small window. It was usually a delivery boy, but with my active imagination, I was afraid that there could be a stranger lurking in one of the shadowy corners waiting to pounce out, or ruffians at the door who might suddenly push their way inside.

Rickety wooden steps led down to the sub-basement cellar. Dim, hanging bulbs barely allowed enough light to maneuver.

Rickety steps in the rear of the house led downstairs to the cellar, a place that proved troublesome for games of hide and seek.

The dirt floor held the smudgy coal bins, and the contents had served as the heat source from an earlier era. Then oil heat replaced coal, and as a result, the whole house was cleaner as coal dust always mysteriously found its way upstairs.

Electric fuse switches were to the right on the wall and on a large board beneath them hung an array of keys on hooks. Some of the round labels were illegible from age; on others, the identification had fallen off. These keys looked as if they might have been original ones from 1860 when the house was built. A few keys were so rusted they never would have fit into a lock. I wondered why Father, so meticulous about other things, did not take the time to put these in order.

The cellar held little interest for Louise or me. Suitcases were stored under the stairs; they invariably needed to be dusted off when brought up for a trip. One autumn our new kitten got lost in the cellar. We could hear her pathetic meowing but she would not come up. I was scared to go down and suggested we place a saucer of milk by the door, but she still was not tempted.

Louise rushed upstairs to fetch flashlights. When she returned she informed me in her bossiest voice, "You are the elder sister and it is your responsibility to go down and find the kitty. I'll wait at the top of the stairs." I dutifully descended. Then, inadvertently, or as a prank, she turned off the light at the exact moment my flashlight gave out. I was so terrified I screamed, so she finally came down to rescue me. We held hands for comfort climbing up the shaky steps. Meanwhile the kitty had scurried up and by the time we returned, it was contentedly rubbing against Nora's leg in the kitchen.

Sometimes we played hide-and-seek with school friends on the maids' day off. Mother would be in her bedroom paying bills or writing letters at her desk. Considering the basement too scary, Louise and I claimed the first floor but urged our friends to use both floors, which provided plenty of splendid hiding nooks.

On the first floor, Louise often fled to the conservatory and tucked herself between the legs of the rattan chair. She moved the pedestal of a drooping fern in front until she was completely hidden. I preferred the long oak Tudor table in the middle of the living room. Unless you bent down and really searched, you missed seeing anyone under there. At the end of the living room, Louise, being slight of build, managed to curl up around the back leg of the tall, carved desk and remain undetected.

Then there was also the telephone closet off the foyer with a door that shut. Our friends never seemed able to locate the light switch so they didn't bother to look in there. In the downstairs coat closet, you could shimmy behind Father's overcoats and sit on the boots.

The dumbwaiter intrigued friends and sometimes someone dared to climb on one of the shelves…but they often waited and waited. The searchers forgot about that as a hiding place, so the hiders often were not discovered and ultimately had to announce themselves after all the fun was finished. One afternoon, we lost my friend Audrey. We called and called but heard no answer. Eventually we found her curled up asleep on the dumbwaiter shelf.

If the hide-and-seek group was large, a few braver friends did venture to the basement. On another occasion, Audrey dragged out the ceiling-high metal drying rack in the laundry room and climbed in, pulling it closed behind her. It wasn't until we were having milk and cookies after the game that we realized she was missing. Searching the basement we heard strange echoing, crying sounds from inside the clothes dryer. It took three of us tugging and tugging to lug it out so she could be released. Audrey then broke into real sobs and we did not know what to do. We hugged and tried to quiet her and pledged new rules of never suggesting friends hide in the basement. We also made

her promise not to tell her mother because we all would get into big trouble.

Louise and I were shaken up by this incident. We realized if Audrey had not gotten out, it could have been serious. I asked Bessie for advice, trusting she would not tell Mother. She listened carefully and said, "Miss Alice, banning the basement for hide-and-seek was a sensible and adult decision to make. You wouldn't want any of your friends to get hurt."

Sometimes a few of us would venture into the carriage house across the garden, which housed our two cars. The remains of Grandfather Hooker's chemistry laboratory were in the other half of the building. The outside windows were grimy with dirt. The wooden door had swollen with time and had to be pushed hard before it fairly flew open, leaving one unbalanced. Even after we clicked on the light switch, the interior was dim and the bulbs dangled from the ceiling on thin cords. I don't think anything had been dusted or cleaned in 30-odd years; whatever we touched soiled our hands. On the second floor where Grandfather did his research stood the stark slate counters. The empty bookshelves and two black leather chairs and sofa in his library looked as though abandoned by ghosts decades earlier.

Louise and I knew that despite its large size, the inhabited parts of the main house at 82 Remsen Street were safe and inviting. However, it seemed wisest not to investigate nooks and crannies that were seldom used: these spaces might hold trouble or harbor hobgoblins.

DISGRACED ON GRACE COURT ALLEY

One afternoon not much was going on at home, so I said to Louise, "Let's go around to Grace Court Alley and see if we can peek inside someone else's carriage house. We only know ours."

In the 1920s, our carriage house had housed Grandfather Hooker's chemistry lab. Now it was a disquieting dark building used for storage of dusty boxes with barely-readable labels. The only time Louise and I went there was to accompany Mother when she got the car out of the garage. She would hoist up the heavy metal door and drive the Chevy out to Grace Court Alley. I stood by the side, then tugged the garage door down and turned the handle to lock it.

Today however, Louise and I skipped off alone down Remsen Street, turned left on Hicks, and stood at Grace Court Alley. It was different from the surrounding neighborhood. I felt uncomfortable on the narrow street without trees; it appeared quite forlorn. People never strolled down Grace Court Alley and you certainly never found children playing in the area. This should have been a message to us, but we were young and blithely forged on.

The two-story brick buildings had ugly metal overhead doors that were difficult to lift up. Some also had ordinary wooden doors beside them. The second-story windows were placed helter-skelter. These coach houses, as they were also called, lacked stoops or stairs to the front doors, and none

had fancy iron fences in front. As soon as we arrived, I wished for the dignity and grandeur of the brownstones a block away.

Cautiously, Louise and I walked on and everything appeared deserted. All the garage doors were clamped shut. Halfway down, I spied one open. I quietly approached and beckoned Louise to follow. She hesitated.

"Shush, this in our opportunity. Just come quickly," I implored.

We stepped into the garage beside a parked car and immediately heard footsteps approaching. We rapidly ducked down behind the car. A woman reached up and pulled down the overhead metal door we had entered until it slammed on the concrete. She turned the black handle to lock it. Then she opened the car door, unloaded her groceries, and we heard her firm footsteps fade as she strode through a door in the back.

Now we were stuck inside with no way to return to the Alley.

"Come on, help me pull this garage door up so we can get out," I bossed Louise in my panic. We reached down to turn the handle, then tugged and tugged on the door but it was too heavy; it just would not budge. So I locked it again and considered our choices.

The garage was dark and smelled of grease. To tell the truth, the place was downright spooky. It was decidedly worse than our carriage house, with Grandfather Hooker's dusty old chemistry lab and slate counters.

We warily walked the length of the building to the wooden door where the woman had disappeared. The doorknob was wiggly but we opened it. We blinked in the sun at a nicely tended garden: a profusion of blooming daffodils with a grassy area and fountain in the middle. Bushes covered with buds were planted around the perimeter. We followed steps leading down to a lower level. Through a window, we watched the cook in her striped uniform and apron putting groceries in the refrigerator. Ten or fifteen minutes had passed and I concluded the woman from the garage probably had gone upstairs to attend to other matters.

"OK, let's go fast," I urged Louise. We scooted full speed across the garden in case someone was looking out an upstairs window. We tapped tentatively on the kitchen door and felt relieved when the cook opened it and smiled at us. "You both look familiar…but however did you children get here?" she asked.

"There's been a terrible mistake," I stammered. "We wanted to see what was inside the carriage house and then the garage door shut and we couldn't get out. I promise we haven't done anything naughty. Could we just run quickly through your back door to go home? And please, please don't mention this to anyone; our Mother would be most upset."

I couldn't believe our good fortune when she asked if we wanted milk and cookies. I frantically shook my head, no. I worried the other woman might come down and scold us.

The carriage house as seen facing Grace Court Alley and from the rear of Remsen Street. It once housed horses, carriages, and grooms as well as Grandfather Hooker's chemistry lab.

The kind cook walked us down a dim hallway to the back kitchen door that opened on Remsen Street and she let us out. I barely turned to thank her as we ran as fast as we could to the safety of our own house.

I felt compelled to swear Louise to secrecy about our mishap: "Now, Louise we aren't going to tell anyone about this adventure. All they'll do is be mad and we really didn't do anything bad."

"Oh, Ali, this was another terrible idea of yours that nearly got us in trouble again. It was a close call. We might have been locked in that scary garage for days with no food or water." Louise was right: it had been a stupid venture and not even fun.

But I was not finished with Grace Court Alley. I knew my sister Louise couldn't be tempted after this last episode. But it wasn't too long before I returned to explore Grace Court Alley on my roller skates.

I sat on our stoop and strapped on my skates, then started out. Of course, there were no cars in the alley. The asphalt was bumpier than I expected. As I skated to the end, I had never noticed the street tilted upward. When I turned around and started back down the slope, I gained more momentum than expected on the decline. I did not want to shoot out into Hicks Street, which was filled with traffic. To slow down now, I had just two choices. I could weave back and forth, which I couldn't seem to manage, or I could throw myself down on the hard street and get all scraped up. I decided to head toward a garage door, put my hands out, and hope for the best. I extended my arms and braced myself. I thumped into the door with a hard jolt and somehow broke off a corner of my right front tooth. The searing pain left me queasy and I sank to the ground crying. I now understood the meaning of "seeing stars." I could feel with my tongue that a large chip had come off my tooth and worried whether the dentist would be able to fix it. I looked around the ground and spied the chip so I put it in my pocket.

For one of the first times in my life, no one was there to feel sorry for me. Next, I became furious at what had happened. Roller skates were my chosen form of transportation around the Heights and they had never let me down. I considered myself completely competent and rarely fell. I had memorized the sidewalks in the neighborhood that had uneven surfaces and I knew how to handle them. I certainly never crashed into anything. Now I had misjudged the slope of the asphalt surface, swerved into the metal door, and damaged my front tooth. I took off my skates, got to my feet, walked home slowly, and did my best to comfort myself. I felt disgraced on Grace Court Alley.

Fishing for Good Humor

During warm weather, Brooklyn Heights' children were acutely attuned to the melodic jingling of the Good Humor Man's white truck. He jiggled the bells hung by the windshield as he got out of his truck. Kids materialized from every cranny near Remsen and Henry Streets clamoring to be first in line.

If I had managed my finances well I could afford this ten-cent treat. But it meant my entire weekly allowance, so I had to forgo any penny candies at Landy's on Montague Street. Sometimes, if I were with Mother, she would agree to pay and dig a dime out from her change purse.

Nothing ever equaled the old-fashioned Good Humor ice cream of 1938. The Good Humor man, dressed in his white uniform and smart cap, would reach over to grab the chrome side door handle of his refrigerated truck. On a warm day, a puff of cold air would come out, so he closed the door quickly. Inside were rows of luscious ice creams stacked on top of each other: vanilla ice cream dipped in thick chocolate coating with a paper wrapping. They were rectangular, round at the top, on a wooden stick.

Ripping off the paper wrapping, I would bite into the chocolate, which split off precariously just before I got the taste of the rich vanilla ice cream. I savored it as slowly as I dared, for if I was too leisurely I ran the risk of the chocolate and ice cream becoming soft and flopping off the stick onto the

Older brother Bob Davidson was very creative when it came to sneaking Good Humor ice creams up to his study.

pavement. Once I even got a "lucky stick," discovered only after I had eaten the ice cream and found the special mark. It meant I got one free ice cream: a cause for rejoicing all day. No friends ever had such good fortune, making my luck all the more unusual.

My older brother Bob, who was thirteen, loved Good Humors especially on warm spring evenings when he could lick one at his desk. Having a larger allowance, he could indulge more often and even called the Good Humor man by his first name: Larry. A problem arose because we were supposed to be in our rooms doing homework at the same time as the vendor's expected arrival. Bob had puzzled this situation through to a solution. He realized that if he brought his fishing reel back from Maine he could enjoy a Good Humor in the privacy of his room. He would arrange with Larry to park in front of the house at precisely 9 p.m., when Mother and Father would be having their after-dinner coffee at the far end of the downstairs living room.

When Bob heard the bells tinkle, he leaned out the window and waved to Larry below. Then he carefully lowered a dime wrapped in a square of paper attached to the fishing gut. Larry removed the dime and tied the Good Humor to the line, crisscrossing it securely. Bob then painstakingly reeled it in like a prize fish, guiding it up as it swung back and forth. He grasped it as it reached the windowsill, and hooted with joy. Then a wave to Larry, who jumped into the truck, gave the bells a last jingle, and sped off.

From my adjacent window I was transfixed by Bob's feat while wondering what the penalty would be if Father found out. Once Bob gave me a bite, and I understood why I had the luck to get even that nibble: this was "hush ice cream," such as "hush money," a payment to keep me from telling our parents. I knew one Good Humor would scarcely be enough for him and did not presume to suggest that he share again in the future. I also never tried to repeat his imaginative maneuver, even after he went off to boarding school and left the fishing rod behind. Somehow, it seemed as though to do so would be infringing on his copyright, and for an admiring sister that would never do.

Storm in a Skiff

Our summer vacations were spent on Sebec Lake in Maine. When we were ready to leave Brooklyn Heights for the summer, Mother and Father packed the Cadillac and the Chevy to the limits and drove in a caravan-type procession that took fourteen hours. Louise, Duke, and I were in the car with Bessie and Nora. Louise and I wiggled, pinched, and swatted each other increasingly as the trip wore on.

Finally, we would arrive at Packard's Camps on Sebec Lake where Mr. Crockett, our genial summer handyman, would wait and greet us with his broad Maine accent. Everyone helped unload the cars and placed the contents in wheelbarrows to take down to the wobbly dock where a small skiff with its eight-horsepower motor was tied. It took three half-hour trips over the lake to get everyone and all our belongings to Greylane Camp, our summer retreat.

Our property consisted of three large buildings: the far log cabin where the maids had their room in the back; the main house with the dining room, kitchen, and bedrooms; as well as the boathouse where Mr. Crockett slept in the front and the boys had bunk beds in the other half.

Sometimes I thought summers consisted of nothing but a daily trip in the skiff to fetch the mail and from there a drive for food supplies at the modest A&P. Rules were strict about boating and swimming as Mother knew how changeable conditions could be on this two-by-twelve-mile lake. I knew I would come of age on the day I'd be allowed to take the skiff alone to pick up the mail.

One afternoon my twelve-year-old brother asked if I wanted to take a trip to Tim's Cove in the motorboat. This was a coveted invitation for a younger sister and so I was thrilled. The afternoon looked fine and the water calm, although I did notice some dark clouds on the distant horizon. We climbed eagerly into the skiff with its six-horsepower motor. I swung the bumpers into the boat and off we drifted.

One pull on the cord and the small outboard motor purred. Bob hugged the shoreline, the better to observe the ledges and woods. We were ever hopeful a long-legged moose or deer might slip down for a sip of cool water. But this never seemed to happen. Instead, we savored the tangy fragrance from the pine trees.

Bob knew the shoreline well; in particular, he knew where the granite rocks came close to the surface. The lake's water level varied over the summer and rocks could suddenly loom closer and become a danger. If our boat propeller scraped a rock, that could put it out of commission or ruin it.

I sat alert in the bow peering into the clear water to warn him of any unexpected boulders lurking below. As we reached Deer Point, he swung in to catch sight of Picnic Rock, which stuck out, and was

Bob and Alice are caught in a reflective moment with a smiling Bebe at their side.

Brother Bob surrounded by his sisters at Sebac Lake in Maine.

magnificently covered with pine needles from the large nearby trees. Our family planned a picnic there once every summer. We would unload bags of dinner mixings, scramble up the granite ledges to the top, start a fire in the outdoor fireplace, and cook our hamburgers and hot dogs.

All seemed serene there, and Bob said he was going to head across the cove to the far point toward the Narrows, quite a distance over the open lake and one we rarely attempted even with adults aboard. This day was still sunny; we both felt euphoric in our independence on this splendid August afternoon.

A half hour later, I cringed to see the sky darkening rapidly, and a strong wind began stirring up the water. Soon the waves were growing in size, and the next thing we knew they were breaking over our bow.

Then the skies opened like a dam. I was soon drenched by the pounding rain. I clung on to both sides of the skiff while edging onto its middle seat. Bob shouted over the wind that he was turning around to head back to camp. Even with making a cautious wide arc, he nearly swamped the boat. The motor began to sputter, and then suddenly stopped. The powerful wind shoved our small boat farther out into the open lake, relentlessly bouncing it around like a cork.

Bracing himself against the tumultuous rocking, Bob reached for the red gas tank and shook it. He took off the cap to peer inside and there was not one drop. Bob was in charge of the boats and had neglected to fill the tank during his morning mail trip to Packard's. Normally he was meticulous about these details concerning the boats. Now I heard him cuss under his breath.

That summer I had been reading a book on miracles and yelled over the wind for him to keep pulling the motor cord: it just might start. Bob tried to no avail. I huddled under an olive green poncho as the raindrops drummed on top of it. The sky was so dark I couldn't see past a few feet or tell in which direction our camp was located. There were no dwellings for miles on Sebec Lake's shoreline. Thunder growled above; I ducked farther under the poncho as lightning etched the sky.

We had been well schooled about the dangers of lightning. I yelled at Bob, "Take your hands off that metal motor and hunker down in the boat."

The boat squeaked and shook as the waves and wind yanked it this way and that. The rain continued to deluge us and I prayed our skiff would not split in two. I was terrified but tried to be brave for Bob. I wasn't sure how long we could last in the water but decided dying would be brief. It crossed my mind that my younger sister Louise might miss me, but would then have all my toys and favorite stuffed animals.

When the rain's deafening chatter softened slightly, I peeked out from under the poncho to find the storm beginning to abate. The sky was brightening in the distance and the lake was gradually losing wave height—as if it had vented all its anger.

We still were way across the lake, but we could just see a dot that might be our camp. The winds had pushed us to the far shore: two miles in what seemed minutes. Bob put in the oarlocks, positioned both oars, and began to row toward the spot.

I looked at Bob as he pulled rhythmically on the oars.

He seemed transformed into a grown man. Though I could see plainly that he was frightened, Bob expressed concern for me: "Are you sure you are OK? Too wet? Too cold? Are you scared? Because I will get you back safely and I promise you we both will be fine." These uncommonly tender words from my older brother were ones I treasured.

The dark descended quickly on the lake as it does in late August, and the night suddenly became chilly. Still, having regained optimism, I climbed back in the bow to direct Bob toward the camp. To our relief, someone had lit the porch light and placed two lanterns on the dock to guide us. I asked Bob if I could help with the rowing, but he assured me he was older and stronger and I was of great help in the bow. I felt wrapped by his concern for me.

Finally, we reached the dock. I threw the bumpers over the side and Bob fastened the boat to the cleats fore and aft. I ran up the path to the porch to assure Mother we were both safe.

There she stood, half-fuming and half-sobbing with relief. I stood there frozen in amazement, not daring to hug her. I struggled to comprehend her reaction; after all, we were the ones on the lake and in danger, she was safe and dry at camp. I was badly in need of a hug and a comforting word, which Mother was unable to muster.

Giving up at last, I went straight upstairs, flung myself on the bed, and sobbed myself to sleep.

Louise tiptoed over to me, put her hand on my shoulder, and said, "Oh, Ali, are you all right? We were all so frightened. Mother never said a word but I knew she was praying. I pulled those six heavy green wooden rocking chairs to the back of the porch alone. Then I put the lanterns on the dock ... I even lit and carried them down all by myself in the pouring rain."

The next day was sunny and the lake tranquil. I ran down to help Bob bail out the skiff. Neither of us said a word but he winked at me when we got the last of the water out.

For years, whenever a fierce storm came up on the lake, Mother recited the remarkable story of five-year-old Louise who pulled the six heavy green wooden rockers to the back of the porch all by herself.

MISCHIEF WITH MINKS

Every year as the holidays approached, there was an accompanying flurry of activity. In preparation for hosting a party, Mother and I had gone to the Fulton Fish Market to select nine Christmas wreaths with puffy red satin ribbons for the windows and large pots of poinsettias. I remember the pungent evergreen smell from the wreaths stacked in the back of the car on the drive home over the Brooklyn Bridge. Mother was excited about the large persimmons that had arrived earlier than usual.

Harry, the man who washed the windows, came the next day to hang the wreaths. First, he fastened wires so he could attach them to steel closures inside. After positioning the wreaths on the second floor, he strode outside to the sidewalk to check that they were all even and hanging properly. He proceeded to the third floor to attach the wreaths there. He hung the last wreath on the front door. The first floor windows were leaded glass with smoky panes and needed no decoration.

My parents were members of the Twentieth Century Club and that evening the club was invited to our house. These evenings were formal with men in tuxedos and women in evening gowns. This was one of the ways Brooklyn Heights' families socialized and kept up on current affairs. Members were nominated and voted in. The evenings were greatly varied and had an educational element. One year the topic might center on literature and another year it could be music or

Alice Hooker Davidson (facing camera) enjoys conversation with guests during one of their frequent dinner parties. Small tables were set up in adjoining rooms to accommodate larger numbers of guests.

political issues. Speakers of note were invited to make presentations.

The evening finally arrived and Mother sat in front of the mirror fixing her hair and dabbing perfume behind her ears. Caterers from Remsen Street had come earlier to set up card tables and chairs for the guests. She expected forty members. Bessie had shined the silver candelabra and put in new twelve-inch white candles. Extra leaves had been added to extend the table to its full length. Bessie had arranged an impressive array of red roses, holly with berries, and white carnations. This centerpiece was placed on the monogrammed white Irish linen tablecloth. Bessie worked hard all week to be sure the house looked its best.

During Mother and Father's dinner parties, we would peek over the staircase to watch the festivities below.

The waiters looked spiffy in black pants, white jackets and gloves. Bessie wore a freshly starched black uniform and white apron and welcomed the caterers. She showed them the pantry and answered their questions. She seemed to enjoy this position of importance.

Louise and I found these occasions exhilarating. We were allowed downstairs for a short while before being hustled off to bed; we put on our brand-new red velvet party dresses with lace collars from Best & Co. The guests usually complimented us generously, amazed at our nice manners and how grown-up we had become.

Earlier, I had sneaked down to the kitchen. Charles, the caterer, was very tall and wore his lofty chef's hat. The main course was to be sweetbreads in a delicious mushroom sauce. He took the lid off the big stainless steel pots, lifted me up to peer in, and then dipped a long-handled spoon in to give me a taste.

"Mmm, so delicate. We never have these unless you come to cater," I remarked, trying to sound like a grownup who dined out frequently.

Next to the huge pot were others: one full of fluffy rice, another with thin-sliced string beans on which Charles sprinkled almonds, and a pot of asparagus. These were all sent up to the pantry on the dumbwaiter with stacks of warmed gold rimmed china plates. The waiters unloaded them in the pantry and took them to the dining room table.

Dessert was my favorite: leaf-shaped chocolate-covered cookies served with dishes of vanilla ice cream and fudge sauce. The cookies remained in shiny, white satin boxes waiting to be arranged on large glass platters. They were more beautiful and tasty than anything I had ever had. Bessie promised to save us a few.

The butler greeted the guests as they came through the door. The men's coats were gently removed and hung in the downstairs coat closet, their black homburg hats lined up neatly on the bench under the window.

The ladies were directed up the wide oak stairs. They lifted their long gowns as they proceeded and I marveled at their fancy strap shoes with high heels.

The women lay their fur coats or shawls on the twin beds in the guest room, sometimes leaving their purses beside them. Louise and I were enthralled. They checked their makeup and remedied any stray hairs; sometimes they made a small adjustment to their dress or tucked in a strap before leaving to join the party downstairs.

The waiters passed fancy hors d'oeuvres arranged artistically on silver platters as the guests stood chatting with their drinks in hand. It all looked formal and smooth and elegant. Louise and I were amused by the extra-polite manners of the guests. The whole scene seemed magical and I wished we could have parties more often.

When the butler announced dinner was served, Louise and I were sent upstairs to bathe and get into our nighties. Bebe helped us carefully hang up our new velvet dresses, and heard our prayers before turning off the light and returning to the kitchen.

But sleepy we were not. Louise and I waited until we knew Bebe was out of earshot. In a daring moment, I suggested we creep out of bed and investigate the guest room where all the women had left their coats.

Our exploration didn't take long to yield results: we opened a few evening bags and found lipsticks, rouge, combs, and change purses. We didn't dare try on the lipstick as we were uncertain how we'd get if off. We stroked the coats and ooh'd and ahh'd over the furs. The minks, which were on top of the pile, seemed the softest. We ventured to try on a few fur hats and paraded around with sequined purses on our wrists.

Louise said in a silly, high-pitched voice, "Oh, dahling, I haven't seen dear Sabrina all fall. Tell her we must arrange tea together." We giggled and told each other how gorgeous we looked.

"Let's climb on the coats and see if they feel springy," I suggested, losing interest in the hats and purses. Getting more adventurous, we walked across the bed of furs and found they tickled our bare feet. This felt so delicious we cautiously began jumping up and down. Gathering courage, we tried leaping from one bed to the other pretending we were circus performers and the coats were our nets.

We became so giddy, we began to whoop and shout: "Hey, hey, hip hooray! Whatever would the guests say?" Oh, how clever we were! Louise miss-stepped and fell, landing on the floor with a thump. She was instantly buried under a mound of fur coats. Delirious with laughter, we dragged them back on the bed and threw ourselves on top of them. Lying on our backs, we kicked our feet and arms in the air like beetles and laughed and laughed.

Suddenly Bebe stalked in. She was quite cross and scuttled us back to our rooms. She was annoyed and scolded us, which was quite unlike her usual demeanor.

Frankly, we theorized that she was piqued about missing the activity in the kitchen. We could picture her eating sweetbreads on a gold-rimmed plate. And when she would ask for seconds of the asparagus and rice, Charles, in his white hat, would gallantly serve her. I always suspected the help experienced more enjoyment than the guests did during these evenings because their daily work was often full of drudgery and their lives held few opportunities for diversion. They knew when to seize light-hearted moments.

The noise downstairs had quieted as the guests settled at the tables to eat. Louise and I could hear the clinking of their forks against the plates and the hum of conversation. Ladies' perfume drifted up to our bedroom and later mingled with men's cigar smoke.

We felt worn out from all the jumping about. We rarely were so mischievous and were lucky Father had not stormed up the stairs two-by-two to spank us with the hairbrush. But even that would have been worth it given all the joy we had bouncing on a bed of mink coats.

CHAPTER 6

Coming of Age

Mirrors and Reflections

One winter after my parents' trip to Florida, Mother returned with a gift for me: a powder compact purse mirror decorated with a pink flamingo standing in front of a palm tree. It probably was purchased in a drugstore. I was young and never understood what had gotten into her. She certainly didn't encourage us to be precocious, so whatever was I to do with this peculiar grown-up accessory?

Mother's own compact was sterling silver with her initials monogrammed on the top surrounded by a square of striated lines. Father had bought it at Tiffany's as a birthday present. Once I noticed a fancy lady at one of our dinner parties take out a gold compact with her initials embedded in diamonds. She had long red fingernails and used a gold cigarette holder when she smoked. But never had I seen a pink flamingo adorning the top of a compact. I think Louise got a pack of playing cards with a flamingo on them, which we immediately put to better use playing crazy eights.

One Sunday the car rearview mirror got me in trouble as we returned from an outing. Stuck in a traffic jam in the Holland Tunnel, Louise and I were in the back arguing about who was hogging more than their share of the seat. We began to elbow each other, and in exasperation, I reached over to pinch her. Father was driving and he adjusted the rearview mirror to observe what was going on. I was caught in mid-pinch and was

roundly scolded, while Louise stuck her tongue out at me. We didn't speak for the rest of the trip home and I was sent to my room early that night.

At home, sneaking small mirrors up to the third floor to outside our older siblings' bedrooms was a favorite activity. We positioned ourselves first and then angled our rectangular mirror by an open bedroom door so we could see what was going on inside. It was a challenge to approach without being heard; we had to creep stealthily and above all, not giggle. Although my siblings were touchy about their privacy and became furious if they detected any intrusion, I don't remember observing anything remotely interesting going on, but it was definitely snoopy and therefore appealed to us.

However, my most dramatic run-in with mirrors was on a rare trip to Coney Island with Mother, Father, and Louise. This was a most unusual expedition for them to undertake: the zoo—yes; the Botanical Gardens or the Brooklyn Museum—yes; but not Coney Island, which seemed far too crowded and public.

We rose early for the trip on a sunny hot day. We loaded the picnic basket with a lunch that Nora had packed and got into the car. After what seemed a long trip, perhaps an hour, we found the parking lot and gathered our belongings. I was stunned at how enormous the beach was: miles and miles of sand with the vast Atlantic Ocean in front. Everywhere was a long walk. Father paid for a locker room where we changed into bathing suits in relays. I had never seen so many people all jammed together on a Sunday afternoon. We strode toward the ocean, managing to find an empty spot large enough to spread our towels not far from the surging surf.

Louise and I ran eagerly to the water but were soon knocked down by the fierce waves and became wary of the strong undertow. So we walked up the beach a bit, always keeping Mother and Father in view. Soon it was lunchtime and we unpacked the tasty chicken sandwiches and cookies. Louise and I had brought checkers to play and so we settled down to a few games. It was not long before we remembered a school friend had raved about the house of funny mirrors at Coney Island. Father and Mother were reading contently, but we were itchy to investigate so we decided to ask one of them to take us. Neither was pleased at having to get up and entertain us, but Father relented. He took each of our hands and asked the lifeguard on his high perch where this mirror house was. The young man pointed in the distance toward the hot dog and ice cream stands.

It seemed a slow walk through the deep sand but finally we spotted the sign. An endless line snaked around to the ticket booth, and after a long wait, Father bought three ten-cent tickets. Dozens of others pushed behind us as we entered. Louise and I were enthralled with our bizarre reflections: tall and skinny, squat and fat, long heads and tiny bodies. Every image was so exaggerated and misshapen. As we continued down the maze moving from one mirror to another, I became confused and somewhat disoriented with these strange misrepresentations.

Kids were laughing and shouting behind me when I noticed Father had disappeared. I looked around in alarm and couldn't locate Louise either. I searched and searched but I couldn't find the way out, as I was pressed deeper and deeper into the mazes. Every time I turned my head, another distorted image reflected back at me. In my apprehension, I gave up and just followed some other kids until we were finally outside in the brilliant sunshine. But where were Father and Louise? They seemed to have vanished, leaving me among the throngs of strangers stretched for miles along the beach. How would I ever find them again? Some people were now packing up their picnic hampers and folding their towels to start back to their cars to beat the homebound traffic.

In which direction should I walk? Where were landmarks I recognized? I knew our towels were by the water but should I go to the left, right, or straight ahead? Seized by terror to be alone in an unfamiliar place and lost in the midst of hordes of strangers, large tears rolled down my face. Everyone around me was busy with his or her ice cream cone or cotton candy; no one noticed how frightened I was.

After what seemed like forever, a kindly policeman walked over and gently asked if I was lost. I began to sob in relief and nodded. He led me to a lost and found place where other children were lost too. An adult comforted me saying they would find my parents. Sometime later Father arrived, visibly relieved to see me. Louise needed to go to the bathroom and he had taken her, and when he returned he couldn't find me.

Mother never realized the trauma that took place during our outing to the house of mirrors. She cheerily packed up our belongings and we found the car to drive home. I was quite exhausted from the sun and scary experience and fell asleep in the car. This must have been a relief for our parents, who for once didn't have to deal with the usual fussing in the back seat.

Fortunately, our time at Sebec Lake in Maine during the summer offered less intimidating reflections. On clear summer days, I loved to stand on the rock ledges by the lake and see myself mirrored in the water. This was especially interesting if a faint breeze rippled the surface and slightly distorted the representation. It was surely less intimidating than the Coney Island trick mirrors.

In my teen years, I found the storefronts with their gigantic glass windows also were handy for checking my profile as I walked down the street. I longed for a full-length mirror on my closet door, a luxury Mother only granted after much persuasion. She had a practical, no-nonsense vision of how we were to present ourselves: attractive and tidy without frills, while making the most of physical attributes with which we were born. Being vain and concentrating on one's looks was foolish; it was far more useful to invest time in developing the mind and character.

Luckily, my Mother eventually agreed and I received a full-length mirror. Harry, the man who washed the Remsen Street windows and hung the Christmas wreaths, drilled the holes in the door to position my new mirror. Evenings I would stand in front of it whirling around, practicing different stances, pretending I was a glamorous actress or a movie star. I visualized myself as a college-aged young woman of limitless sophistication in a 1920's white strapless evening gown with a train, blowing smoke rings from a cigarette in a long holder. Two handsome young men would stand by my side, savor every word I uttered, and beg to dance with me.

Foxtrots at Miss Hepburn's Dancing School

Sandy was long-legged, rosy-cheeked, and when dressed in his gray flannel trousers with a navy jacket, the best-looking boy in Miss Hepburn's Dancing School. He was friendly to everyone and a great dancer too. Standing there awkwardly in my new green dress of soft French velvet, I wondered whether any boy would choose me, or would I have to dance with one of the girls again.

Unbelievably, Sandy strode over, bowed, and asked if he might have the dance. He gently offered his hand with its long fingers and led me to the dance floor. Putting his arm around me in proper dance position, I felt him press his hand on my back a little more than necessary, and he grinned as I looked at him. He offered an open, unembarrassed smile as if he was enjoying my company. A shiver of pleasure went through me as we started the fox trot—step, together, step, together—just as Miss Hepburn or Miss Cargill, her assistant, had taught us. There was no shuffling with heavy feet, nor stumbling. We were in sync: our feet were skimming the floor transported to a place where one moves effortlessly to the beat of the music. With his smooth lead, this was the most glorious experience I had ever had. Feeling irresistibly glamorous, I could hardly breathe from excitement as he pulled me closer.

Miss Hepburn was 5-feet tall and strangely thin in her sweeping 3-foot 4-inch-long black dress, and ten-button suede gloves that reached her elbows. Her black hair was pulled back in a fashionable bun fastened with a puffy bow, and too youthful, I thought, for her middling years. The striking thing about her was the black satin stiletto-thin high heels in which she pranced. In contrast, Miss Cargill was tall and looked like an Art Deco model, favoring black satin high-heeled shoes with straps. She chose one of the girls and swished her startled young partner around the dance floor interspersing the steps with fancy dips.

I looked down at my patent leather flats and stockings held up by a new garter belt; they seemed so daring an hour earlier. Suddenly I was filled with pubescent insecurities: I felt too plump, dumpy, and ugly in the dress.

Miss Hepburn's Dancing School was the rite of passage for the children in Brooklyn Heights. The mothers were delighted when she accepted their offspring, first tentatively through an invitation, and then followed by an interview. If an older sibling belonged, the next in line automatically was on the list. The girls, fifth to eighth grade, were ecstatic at the thought of party dresses and new shoes; the boys groaned and complained about having to wear Sunday clothes just to go through the tedious ritual of learning to dance. Lessons ran from September to late May, and during that time we would have learned the fox trot, the waltz, the lindy, the Lambeth walk, and other popular dance steps that would prepare us for later debutante parties, usually held during the Christmas season freshmen year at college.

As we arrived promptly at 4:30 p.m. each Friday at the Brooklyn Women's Club on Pierpont Street opposite Monroe Place, Miss Hepburn and Miss Cargill greeted us individually at the door, shaking our hands. The girls were to curtsy and the boys to bow slightly from the waist in a manly fashion. In the ballroom, plain folding chairs were lined up along both sides of the wall, the girls to sit on the right and the boys on the left. Students mingled, but in reality stood about in same-sex groups laughing and posturing uneasily. The boys told jokes while the girls giggled in a flirtatious way. On the dance floor, partners were to converse on such subjects as school, sports, and current events. After each dance the boys were expected to pour their partner water in paper cups lined up on the far table.

Miss Hepburn dramatically held her hands over her head and clapped her castanets for silence and then asked the boys and girls to sit on their usual sides. She announced a review of the fox trot and demonstrated this with a short boy who looked like he would die right then and there. As she turned around to put the needle on the phonograph record, five of the boys surreptitiously took off for the men's room with pockets full of marbles, where they planned to hang out for most of the class.

The choosing of partners commenced, the boys shuffling and holding back, hesitant

Miss Hepburn's dance classes were held at 114 Pierpont Street in what was then the Brooklyn Women's Club. Photo by Henrik Krogius

about picking a girl. The girls waited silently, praying someone, any boy, would come and ask them to dance. The wallflower syndrome started early. Miss Hepburn did not want any "pairing up," as if that might lead to a dangerous liaison. The boys could only ask a girl to dance *once*. In the Heights, families sent their children to the girls' school, Packer, or the boys' school, Poly Prep. There was little opportunity for the boys and girls to meet, unless a best friend introduced you to their sisters or brothers.

After overseeing the young people in the room, getting them properly paired off and on the dance floor, Miss Hepburn stormed off to the men's room, with long strides used only on this occasion. She pounded on the door and sternly told the boys to pick up their marbles and unlock the door or she would have to go in and drag them out. There were muffled guffaws, but nonetheless, they were awed by Miss Hepburn and the power she held over their lives. The boys opened the door and filed out stifling their laughter.

Expulsion from her classes was a cause for shame, and worse, fury from their parents. The boys said they didn't want to be there, but missing out on the girls and the fun was even worse. So in a silent pact, they agreed to come, cooperate (to a degree), spend some time protesting with marbles in the men's room, and then reluctantly join the class again.

The foxtrot eventually ended at this particular Friday's dance, and Sandy, his face slightly flushed, released his arm from my back leaving a warm tingling feeling. We continued chatting as he escorted me to the table for a cup of water before taking me to my folding chair. He bowed smartly, gave me a wink, and returned to the boys' side of the room. Eighth grade was a glorious year with Sandy choosing me for one dance every single class. My lifelong love of dancing started that very day in the green velvet dress.

CALAMITY AT KITTY'S DEBUTANTE BALL

One of Mother's more challenging enterprises was my sister Kitty's debutante party during the 1939 Christmas holidays. Kitty was a freshman at Vassar, Louise and I were still in grade school, and our brother Sidney attended Yale.

Kitty and Sidney both had friends in the Heights, at college, and in the cross-cultural exchange program known as the Experiment in International Living. The guest list would also include a sprinkling of Mother and Father's Heights friends. Sidney assured an ample supply of young Yalies.

Seating around the edge of the living room and in the conservatory would allow everyone a view of the festivities. Sofas and many armchairs had to be shifted to the wall. Three hefty men strode in the morning before the party. They pulled and shoved the furnishings around. To clear the floor required tugging the heavy oak rectory table from the middle to the side, then rolling up the Oriental rug, which stretched the length of the room. The men rolled up the enormous rug as if it were a bathmat, leaving the Turkish walnut floor free for dancing. The whole living room was transformed by noon. I had never witnessed this daunting task before, and I was a bit unnerved to see our home so converted. The space echoed like a cavern with no rugs to buffer the sound.

Louise and I raced around clicking our heels on the bare wood floor. I spied a few pennies and my favorite silver bracelet, lost

Older sister Kitty's debutante ball was a splendid occasion despite an unexpected incident on the stairs. Photo by Drummond Co. Photographers

the year before. Louise found her barrette. Bessie rushed in with the mop to take care of any dust or debris that was hidden under the carpet.

Earlier Mother had taken Kitty on a shopping trip to New York. At Lord & Taylor's they found a gorgeous white strapless gown with green piping on the front and a full skirt, rather daring for the time. I gasped with delight when she modeled it, quickly counting the years until I might wear it. The

Kitty takes refuge in a tree in a playful moment.

dress would show off her shoulders and thick dark hair, which would hang in silken tresses the night of the party.

Sidney seemed indifferent about the plans but was a natural on the dance floor, having mastered the steps at Miss Hepburn's Dancing School. His 6-foot 2-inch height was perfect for the taller girls; he relished the livelier ones and savored the event.

Hill's Catering consented to supply everything, including the dinner, the waiters, the card tables, and chairs. This affair included music and dancing, which meant a violinist, a violist, and a drummer.

The debutante party night arrived with the usual bustle: stainless steel pots of food arriving through the basement entrance, the butler and waiters dressed in their tuxedos. Everyone was cooperating perfectly, with one exception: Greta, our substitute cook, was growing increasingly irritable. Nora, our regular cook was on a six-week vacation in her homeland of Ireland. The employment agency had sent Greta as a temporary replacement. Mother had found her cooking satisfactory so Greta was scheduled to remain until Nora's return the following week.

On this special night Louise and I were not welcome in the kitchen, so we spied on Greta as she mumbled and hustled around, shaking a wooden spoon in the air. That evening Greta had adamantly refused to leave the house, conceding sullenly to retire to her third-floor bedroom.

Mr. Roberts, the butler, greeted the arriving guests: gorgeous young women in gowns of every color, young men in handsome tuxedos. I had never seen such a transformation of the girls, from their plaid skirts and Shetland sweaters to this. They even wore a little make-up and perfume. Louise and I vowed to see this to the finish— no going to bed early tonight. We wanted to register every detail, knowing someday we would reach this magical age. A young man might even dance with us. My sixth sense questioned whether such an evening would be repeated.

Everything started out as planned. After sherry, the guests went to the buffet, selected from the plates of roast beef, lobster bisque, and other delicacies, and sat at the card tables chattering gaily with their partners. Many of the younger guests preferred to stand, eating as they circulated around. The older guests were mostly in the conservatory, less conspicuous but able to see everything.

Then the music began. The girls looked radiant as the young men asked them to dance and the room became a swirl of colors. The men were cutting in to dance with Kitty, who whirled from one to another with barely a few dance steps with each. Yvonne, from Paris, was visiting her aunt on the Heights; she wore a stunning gown trimmed with black lace reportedly made by Balenciaga, who someone said was an important designer. My favorite cousin, Polly Davidson, who attended Wellesley College, wore a sequined red gown with daring spaghetti straps. Most of the girls wore pearls and one had a diamond clip in her new short hairstyle.

Even Mother and Father danced. Sarge Shriver, John Walker (he later married Kitty), and other young men took Mother on a twirl around the floor. She looked younger than I ever remembered in her royal blue lace dress and velvet strap shoes.

First, the dancers did the fox trot to "Polka Dots and Moonbeams" and "Deep Purple." Then the next thing we knew everyone was chasseing up and down to a lively polka as the band's momentum increased. By then, all the girls were on the dance floor—no wallflowers tonight. One girl caught her heel in the hem of her gown,

but her partner steadied her and she quickly regained her equilibrium. Soon the room was filled with flapping arms as some did the Charleston, followed by others jitterbugging so fast that you could scarcely see their feet flying about.

Next, Louise and I were astonished when Sidney asked Kitty to dance. He stepped out, took the lead, and they waltzed so smoothly the guests stood aside to watch. Her white skirt whirled as if lifted round in a breeze. Up and back the length of the living room they went, three, four, five times until the music slowed. I'd never seen anything so effortless and splendid. Louise and I concluded they must have been practicing on their own… and I wondered how I'd missed that.

Couples were holding hands as they stood together waiting for the music to begin. Louise and I heard some giggling in the hallway and tiptoed out to glimpse a twosome stealing kisses beneath the grandfather clock's watchful eye. We delighted in watching the flirtations.

As the night continued, Louise alerted me to some turmoil on the third floor: Bessie rushed in to whisper something urgent in Mother's ear. Mother left suddenly and hastily started up the stairs with Louise and myself right on her heels. Greta, looking wild-eyed, was on her way down with a long knife, screaming, "I can't sleep with all this dreadful noise! Everyone has to leave the house immediately! Get that cook with his silly hat and big pots out of my kitchen!

He is in my territory! Tell those wretched waiters in their fancy clothes to go home! It's like an invasion and I won't have it!"

Mother said in her no-nonsense voice, "Put that knife down instantly and sit on the stairs." Greta dropped the knife, flopped down on the step without a word, and helplessly stared at Mother. Mother turned to Bessie, "Call the police department. Emphasize we have an emergency. We need two officers. Tell them to turn off the flashing light on the car. Have them come through the basement entrance, and then use the servant's stairs in the pantry so the guests won't see them. Above all, we mustn't disturb Kitty's party."

As luck would have it, Bebe's husband Patrick was on duty and arrived with another policeman, both in uniform with truncheons. The two men conducted themselves flawlessly. By the time of their arrival, Greta appeared calmer; they took her downstairs and to the hospital without any fuss. Louise and I watched in awe as Mother straightened up, walked down both flights of stairs, and returned to the party as if nothing had happened.

With this drama over, Louise and I flew back downstairs to see how the party was progressing. A kind Yale freshman danced with each of us, probably just a few awkward steps, but I chatted gaily and lifted my face up in a beguiling way that I had noticed the young women do. Someday I too would spin up and down a dance floor.

Louise and I finally went off to bed at midnight while the musicians played "Good Night, Ladies." We could hear the guests collecting their coats and expressing appreciation for the party. We assumed there were more stolen kisses that night and trusted that we could handle them too when our own turns came.

The Dance Ended too Soon

Late fall had come when Mother and my friends' mothers, Mrs. McKee and Mrs. Foote, met to discuss the logistics of the debutante tea dance for their daughters. The coming-out party was a rite of passage for young women of the time. It signified a coming-of-age and that she was ready to be presented to society: the adult community and eligible young men. Our party would be an afternoon tea dance rather than an evening debutante ball.

The three mothers decided the New York Junior League premises would be the best place to hold this event; a small Lester Lanin band would provide music. The reservations had been made a year in advance. Each family would ask thirty young people, plus adult friends. Of course, the list overlapped because our families had many friends in common.

A week later, a Tiffany's truck pulled up in front of our house and a deliveryman, smartly dressed in livery and leather boots, brought the blue boxes of invitations and envelopes. They were engraved on Tiffany's heavy ivory stock with a reply enclosed. Mother invited Mrs. Foote and Mrs. McKee for an afternoon at our house to address them on our dining room table.

I remember seeing the three of them with reading glasses perched on their noses, heads bent to seriously attend to the task. They resembled students rather than mothers. Each parent had brought a final guest list

The author photographed as a young Vassar student.

and spent the afternoon together addressing the invitations in exemplary handwriting. They even agreed upon which stamps to use.

Exactly at 4 p.m., Bessie brought in the silver tea tray. Mother paused to fill the cups, inquiring whether they preferred their tea weak or strong. Bessie passed the cream and sugar as well as the plate of ornate Ebinger's petit fours.

The stickiest challenge we debutantes had was to decide which boys might accompany us. We each needed three escorts and were unnerved to telephone the boys ourselves. Many young men were not interested in this type of occasion. "I don't want any boy snickering on the telephone when I extend my invitation," I said to Patty Foote.

I struggled and struggled over whom to call. My acquaintanceship with boys was limited; we all went exclusively to girls' schools: Packer, Vassar, or Mt. Holyoke. We had met only a few boys at Yale, Harvard, and nearby colleges during our first semester away. I was the only one with a brother, and Bob, five years older, was elsewhere that Christmas vacation.

I knew I wanted only tall escorts, none of those shrimpy, short boys who just reached my shoulder, leaving me with my head wagging in the wind. They needed to be well mannered, preferably a year or so older, and passable dancers. I couldn't be too fussy about the latter because I remembered only two boys from Miss Hepburn's class who were adept on the dance floor and Jeannie McKee had already spoken for Peter Everson.

The thought of three escorts thrilled me; I envisioned them constantly cutting in and vying for my attentions on the dance floor. I planned to instruct them that their duty that evening was to look solely after me and dance with me several times. I did not want to sit out any dance, let alone risk being seen as a wallflower.

Then there was the question of an evening dress. I knew I wanted my first off-the-shoulder gown as I fancied I had fetching shoulders and arms that needed to be shown off. Mother and I headed for B. Altman's and within an hour, we found the perfect gown at the right price. It was white taffeta that rustled as I moved, with a red velvet trim around the top of the bodice. How sumptuously it fit, not too tight, plenty of room to dance and swirl around the floor, with no danger of the bodice slipping.

Mother bought me a saucy pair of medium-heeled shoes that were unusually comfortable. At the glove department on the first floor, Mother also purchased a pair of French eight-button soft kidskin gloves to complete my outfit. I felt giddy with so many exquisite clothes purchased in one day.

Excitement mounted as December 29 came closer. Usually Christmas was the highpoint, but this event outshone everything.

Two days before the party, twenty-five inches of snow began to fall, tangling all transportation. The city became immobilized by the massive snowstorm. Trucks and cars were stuck in the street, no taxis were available, and the subways ceased running. Mother told Louise only three guests had declined.

By the day of the party, the subway was running again and there were narrow paths winding up and down the sidewalks. We packed our dresses in suitcases and pushed our way through the wind and falling snow to Borough Hall to take the subway to 50th and Lexington. We trudged through more snow until we reached the Junior League's premises, where I shook out my snow-filled boots. We changed into our finery to carry on with the debutante party.

We formed a long line: each mother, father, and debutante daughter stood to shake hands with every guest. A sense of adventure prevailed at the party as guests had arrived despite such weather conditions. Nonetheless, everyone was meticulously turned out in evening attire: we three debutantes in the requisite white gowns, the men in their black tuxedos. The mothers favored lace dresses of all colors with little jackets.

The receiving line finally broke up and one of my escorts, Sandy, took my hand for the first dance. Oh, how we whirled and twirled with my dress swinging out as we covered the floor. Then David cut in, and though not as skilled a dancer, his repartee was always amusing. Next, Rob told me I looked alluring and was the prettiest girl there. He said how honored he was to be asked as my escort. He whispered some other sweet things in my ear as we danced cheek to cheek but I was too exhilarated to hear them.

Lester Lanin played all my favorite tunes: "People Will Say We're in Love," "Shall We Dance," "Just Give Me Five Minutes More," many from popular Broadway musicals of the time.

The next, the next, and the next boy cut in; I only had a few steps with some before a young gentleman's tap on the shoulder, and off I would twirl with a new partner. I'd never felt so glamorous or popular and something inside me realized it might never happen again.

I was breathless when the band took a short break and we headed for the food table. I even sipped a small glass of wine. I gathered my escorts around me and divulged that I wanted more dances with each, so off we went again. Everything became smoother and smoother; my face was flushed and I knew I could have continued long into the night. By now, the adults were on the floor doing a round or two in a more staid way. All my friends were dancing, as were the "extra" boys eager to show off their prowess.

A bit of spirited jitterbugging energized everyone and a polka sent us galloping around the perimeter of the room. Then back to the foxtrots and rumbas. My feet moved magically, following wherever my partners led me. What a success! No despondent girl on the sidelines wishing for a partner....

The band played one last tune and suddenly the party ended. I could not believe it as it felt to me that we had just begun. All of the boys in attendance had put aside their shyness, exhibited their best manners, and acted courtly and flirtatious. Each escort hugged me tightly with a friendly kiss on the cheek.

In bed that night, I counted every single boy who had danced with me and then re-counted, in case I had missed some. If this was the beginning of adulthood, I knew I was willing to meet the challenge with zest.

CHAPTER 7

End of an Era

A Bomb Drops

I will never forget the moment. It was December 1941 and my oldest sister Jean and I were in her bedroom chattering away as she helped me with a dropped stitch. I was knitting a woolen scarf to be sent overseas for the refugees. The music on the radio stopped abruptly and the announcer said, "The Japanese have bombed Pearl Harbor." We didn't know where Pearl Harbor was but we were stunned. The next day President Roosevelt declared war and announced the country would have to mobilize rapidly.

One morning life was normal and by the next morning, everyone was plagued with worries and questions. Numerous phone calls were placed to my brothers Bob and Sidney at Yale. Serious irreversible decisions needed to be made and quickly. Should they drop out of college and join the Army or Navy or wait until they were called? Should they enlist immediately or go to officers' training school? This was later to be called "The Good War" because no one questioned that everyone was going to do his or her part. Bob wanted to work on a submarine; Mother thought that ridiculous with his 6-foot 4-inch height. He ended up in the Navy. Sidney went to an aircraft carrier in the Pacific. Jean announced she wanted to join the WAVES, the women's division of the U.S. Navy. To me this seemed a daring thing for her to do.

My favorite cousin, Douggie Davidson in Delaware, enlisted immediately as a medical

The author's mother, Alice H. Davidson, bids farewell to her son Sidney W. Davidson, Jr. as he leaves to sign up for Navy officers' training school.

paratrooper, knowing if he waited, he would not be accepted because of his 6-foot 5-inch height. He later set the criteria for height and weight of paratroopers, causing measurements to be lowered to 6-feet 4-inches and 190 pounds. This was presumably so they wouldn't strain the parachutes and fall too rapidly. He had to lose thirty pounds

Ensign (later lieutenant) Jean Davidson, the author's oldest sister, stands in her WAVE uniform with the man who became her husband, Jack Fay, an Army Air Corps major who flew a B-29 in the Pacific as that service branch developed into the Air Force.

than twenty-five cents for the duration of the war. This was our personal sacrifice and one we gladly would make for the war effort.

By spring, young men on the streets in uniform looked transformed. They had straight postures and walked with a purpose. Some wore officer's hats with visors; overseas caps were worn at certain angles; jackets had stripes on the shoulders; trousers were creased and shoes were shined. The pilots looked dashing in their brown leather bomber jackets. I saw Neil Taylor, a family friend, at a wedding in the red, white, and blue Marine dress outfit and concluded it was the snappiest of all.

Jean became a new ensign in the WAVES and wore her navy blue skirt, white shirt, and a jacket with a gold stripe on her shoulders. I liked walking beside her because the enlisted men stopped, stood at attention, and saluted her smartly. She acknowledged the salute with one of her own. On return from church one Sunday, a young sailor did not immediately render the customary salute and she spoke to him sharply. I was surprised at her authority.

New posters went up in store windows and subway cars: Uncle Sam with his patriotic top hat, pointing his long finger, "I Want *You*!" or a picture of two people talking with a zipper across their lips, "Zip your lips, spies may be listening."

At the St. George Playhouse, where we went for fifteen-cent Saturday matinees, a short film featured plump Mayor LaGuardia. He instructed us how to put out an incendiary bomb by pouring water on it.

himself to meet his own regulations. (As a captain in France toward the end of the war, Douggie carried a white flag to the German lines to invite their surrender.)

There was both fear and eagerness to participate in the war effort. No one understood his or her role, but everyone tried to figure out how to help. My sister Louise and I held a solemn pow-wow and decided our allowance should not be raised more

It was later realized this would make it spread—what was needed was sand.

Changes occurred at home: Nora still was our cook, but mother took longer conferring with her about meals. Rationing had begun and meals became simpler but were still nutritious. There was less meat and fewer choices of cuts; we ate more thick soups, and the breads seemed heartier. Nora was clever at stretching things so the food remained tasty; I think she covered up a lot with sauces. Butter and sugar were rationed so desserts became more modest. Cakes and cookies became rare treats. The comforting ritual of afternoon tea was continued and mother occasionally had friends in, especially the Haynes sisters on the corner of Remsen and Hicks Streets who had no children and were interested in our family. Mother still poured from the silver teapot and Paul Revere hot water jug, which were kept shined as usual on the silver tea tray. Instead of home-baked cookies, we had plain bread with jam.

It took longer now to do the errands on Montague Street as women stopped to exchange news of their sons and to try to reassure each other everyone would return home safely.

The A&P on Atlantic Avenue and other markets had less produce from which to choose. Mother became adept with ration coupons; there were lines waiting to get scarce items. Victory gardens became popular; anyone with a small plot of land grew vegetables and canned jars of beans, beets, and carrots to see them through winter.

The upstairs maid left to work in the munitions factory, so we all pitched in washing dishes in the pantry after meals. I rather liked the novelty at first—Father, doing his part, designated himself the dishwasher. He ceremoniously took off his jacket, rolled up his sleeves, and stood by the stainless steel sink. He looked comical with a dishtowel around his waist and his hands immersed in the sudsy water. We vied to take turns wiping the dishes but never established a schedule to assign each person responsibility for certain nights. After the first week, Father became impatient and bossy and we wished he would let us do the job and go back to reading *The Sun* in his leather chair in the living room. But he insisted....

Gas was rationed so we only took our car out on weekends. Father was meticulous about following rules, with one exception: he hoarded extra tires realizing rubber would be in short supply. I counted eight new tires piled in a corner of the basement. He seemed rather proud of his foresight but I deemed it unpatriotic.

Late one night Louise and I crept out of bed in our pajamas and sat at the top of the stairs eavesdropping: Mother and Father were weighing the pros and cons of moving to our farm in Pottersville, New Jersey. There was speculation that New York might be bombed, and so the farm outside of the city seemed safer. The hundred-acre farm was just thirty miles from the city and Father could still commute by train to Wall Street.

In the past, we would drive to the farm on weekends and spent the previous summer there too. My sister Louise and I loved it, although it seemed to take forever to drive with traffic creeping through the Holland Tunnel, while Duke, the cats, Louise, and I fussed impatiently in the back seat.

The spacious farmhouse could easily accommodate our large family and guests. From the upstairs window, we viewed fertile undulating fields, the farmer's cottage to the south, then the barn and the chicken house.

Although Louise and I were not keen about leaving our Brooklyn Heights' friends, but when the time came, we accepted Mother and Father's decision to go. Not long thereafter, we reluctantly began packing our favorite Remsen Street belongings not knowing how long we would be gone.

Family Farming Abridged

We shut the Remsen Street house when we moved to Pottersville during the war. Although weekends and summers at the farm had been an adventure, Louise and I were reluctant to leave Packer and embrace a new country routine. Our new school was in Bernardsville and required a long drive twice a day. I missed the freedom of walking to Packer with friends and seeing Officer Butler and his horse Gallop when we returned afternoons.

At the farm, we had one cow and Mother bought me a black lamb, which I named Clover. That lamb followed me everywhere. Even though I trained her on a leash, Mother forbade me to bring her in the house. When I had Clover sheared, I learned to spin the wool and knit a scarf and mittens, which I proudly showed off to my classmates. Louise felt left out and begged for her own lamb, which she named Spooky. Once Spooky arrived, Clover immediately shunned me, preferring her new woolly companion. I was cross at Louise that entire week.

That spring Father decided to increase production at the farm. He did not really understand agriculture nor was he prepared for the snags. My father loved artistic order so when we added another cow, some heifers, a few pigs and chickens he chose black and white breeds so they would blend with the farmhouse's color scheme. As we drove in, our eye caught the white farmhouse with black shutters complemented by black animals grazing in the green pastures.

The government put out reams of regulations in small print that included how

To match the white house with black shutters in Pottersville, New Jersey, Sidney W. Davidson decided that all the livestock should be black and white.

The author feeds a calf that somehow escaped the black-and-white rule.

the land was to be used. This required reading rules and filling out reports, which Father did on weekends in his tiny farm office off the kitchen. My father had little patience when things did not go as planned, so farm life became a burden to his already busy law practice. But Louise and I enjoyed the series of unpredictable experiences in which we could be involved.

We ordered lively, fluffy chicks from Macy's that arrived the next day. We picked them up at the general store, which also served as a post office. Louise and I gingerly lifted the large, unwieldy cardboard box, careful not to tilt it and let the chicks slide to one end trampling each other. Through holes in the top, we could hear timid peeping chirps. The first group of chicks

contracted coccidiosis and died. So we ordered more from Macy's again.

Once the chicks grew up and started laying, they were successful until they took weeks off for molting and stopped producing. Consequently, many found their way to the kitchen pot to become chicken fricassee. Louise and I constantly checked the hen house and collected the eggs, snatching them from under the birds' feathery bellies. Giving us the beady eye, the hens cackled crossly as we retrieved each warm egg. Carrying the eggs to the barn in our wire mesh baskets, we would clean them and place them in tin flats holding forty-eight eggs. Sometimes Father would send them to friends or relatives. They could be delivered to the city by overnight mail, every one arriving without a crack.

Bossy the cow did her part supplying us with milk, until suddenly her production fell: we discovered the new Black Angus heifers were helping themselves to her milk, so they were quickly moved to another pasture.

As we added more animals, we needed winter fodder, so Father had several fields planted with alfalfa. The first crop grew quickly and I remember our excitement as Jim, the farmer, revved up the tractor and spent hours cutting the hay. Then he left it in the field for a few days to dry in the sunshine. The sweet scent wafted everywhere, and made us realize that we were really farming.

The morning Louise and I heard the tractor shifting gears in the field below our bedroom window; we dressed quickly and rushed out to help. Young hired hands hefted the heavy rectangular bales tied with two strings, then tossed them onto the wagon to be taken into the barn. Louise and I clambered onto the prickly bales, trying mightily to push them in place. In reality we must have been a nuisance, not strong enough to hoist the bales and always underfoot. Often the tractor groaned forward with a jerk as we nearly lost our balance. However, we were not going to miss this important operation.

Later in the summer, at dusk and after all the fieldwork was completed, Louise and I would unlatch the heavy barn doors. Both of us had to tug them open—just enough to peek in and get a heady whiff of the hay. Hundreds of bales piled layer-by-layer, awaited winter. Sometimes we caught a glimpse of the black barn cat poised to pounce on a mouse.

The sows bore litters of eight to a dozen piglets but often rolled over and smothered some. Turkeys were difficult because they were susceptible to so many diseases, including pneumonia from wet feet. Several dozen died in two days. When they were kept off the ground in large wire cages, more reached adulthood.

Louise and I named all the animals, and felt sad when our favorites were hauled off to the butcher. We named the pigs after handsome friends of our older brothers and were puzzled when none seemed flattered by such an honor.

The author's mother, Alice H. Davidson, loved to garden, and as always, wore the proper hat for the occasion.

The animals were trucked to the butcher where Mother designated which cuts of meat she preferred, including how many pounds of chopped meat. The butcher kept a percentage as his fee. Everything was frozen instantly and kept in his commercial freezer until we transferred it to our smaller one. Home freezers were new to the market and were large rectangular chests with removable trays inside and a heavy lid. Father had gotten the last one at the farm supply store, and everyone was very pleased with it.

Each time a pig was slaughtered, an ongoing discussion ensued about the flavor of the sausage. Father liked a delicate taste and others favored it stronger. He insisted it be in patties rather than encased in the ugly intestine.

As the war continued, additional foods were rationed; frozen goods had not yet come on the market. Canned vegetables required coupons, and tasted tinny, so more attention was bestowed on the Victory garden of vegetables, which flourished. Each morning Louise and I headed out with our straw hats to weed. The berries grew prolifically. They were my favorite to pick, especially the tasty raspberries and large juicy black boysenberries, a recent hybrid. We took our full baskets into the kitchen and put the berries in clear plastic bags, another novelty. Then Mother sealed them with a machine before putting them in the freezer.

Father, a radish lover, did not realize that three long rows would feed the countryside. We couldn't begin to eat that many, so we carried them to the local general store to sell or gave them to friends in the city. My Father learned what many Victory gardeners realized: farming is a profession like any other, requiring a delicate balance of vast knowledge and experience.

Finally, we needed gas for everything: Mother became a chauffeur—driving Father to the train station, leaving and picking us up from school. Father was exhausted from the commute and I wondered if he missed the exercise of walking the Brooklyn Bridge to Wall Street. As quickly as we had moved out, we returned to the Heights some weeks later.

War's Reality Reaches the Heights

I cannot remember shopping for new clothes during the war. However, the dressmaker did come to the house and sewed a few dresses for my younger sister Louise and me out of Liberty cotton fabric that Mother had bought some years earlier. Mother also rummaged through older siblings' closets to find appropriate replacements for clothing we had outgrown. Clothing choices in the retail stores also were limited, as manufacturers now were geared to making uniforms for the military.

Mother did not buy anything new for herself: no hats from Miss Francoise or new suits or dresses. We always seemed to be taking in or letting out dresses and coats.

Shoes were rationed to one pair a year per person. In 1945, my friend's mother passed her ration coupon on to Mother so she could buy a new pair of shoes for graduation ceremonies at Packer.

Father had given Mother a skunk jacket the year before, which she considered quite fashionable. Although she had hoped to preserve it for special occasions, she now wore it all season. I remember after a few winters of snow and rain, the fur began to smell; as it became matted, the true origin of the beast revealed itself. The unpleasant acrid odor went through the downstairs coat closet, tainting my Sunday blue woolen coat with velvet collar from Best & Co. When World War II ended and luxuries were obtainable, the skunk jacket finally disappeared and no one was more delighted than I was.

Jeannie McKee and I used to traipse down to the Long Island College of Medicine to roll bandages on Saturday mornings. We felt grown-up walking down Henry Street with classmates, going through those big doors and taking the elevator to the fourth floor. There we settled down around a rectangular table, gossiping and visiting like adults. We washed our hands but did not wear plastic gloves, which had not been invented. Bandages were in short supply and this was considered an important gesture to support the war effort.

One handsome young man in the neighborhood was in the Office of Strategic Services (OSS), a precursor of the CIA. He wore civilian clothes and kept his profession a secret, so the wives and mothers badgered him relentlessly: "My son is offering his life to serve his country, how dare you avoid the draft." He always looked them coolly in the eye and said: "But I have a venereal disease and they won't take me." With that any discussion ended. He thought these incidents amusing, but I was proud of him for being in such a dangerous branch and thought his role should be appreciated more.

After Sunday services at the Unitarian Church, Mother often invited one or two servicemen for dinner whose ships were awaiting departure. Our long oak table was still set with a white linen tablecloth and silver settings, the cut glasses were filled with ice water. Meats and frozen vegetables were brought in from Brookfield Farm; Louise and I were relieved that we couldn't identify which favorite animal we were eating that day.

I thought it wonderful to have these brave sailors with us. At the time, they seemed like men but in reality were just a few years older than Louise and me. Some of them came from small towns across the country that we did not know and they pointed out their locations on maps. They often showed us photos of their mothers, fathers, and girlfriends.

We had a constant stream of guests who stayed with us, as the young men shipped out from the Brooklyn Navy Yard. The guestroom was my favorite room in the house with its high ceiling, marble fireplace, four-poster twin beds, and mahogany bureaus. My cousin Polly Davidson came; her new husband Ray had graduated from Harvard recently and he had been assigned to a naval destroyer. She had just finished junior year at Wellesley College. She arrived from Delaware to see him off.

Ray would arise at 5 a.m. and tiptoe down the stairs to report to the Brooklyn Navy Yard. Every morning as he quietly clicked the front door shut, I would hear Polly crying in bed. We had poignant meals each night, knowing his departure time would eventually come. For ten evenings, he reappeared at suppertime as the Navy assembled the twenty-odd ships for the convoy. Finally, Mother said, "Ray, we aren't going to say goodbye anymore, because you keep coming back." Then, the eleventh morning, he called Polly from a pay phone, which was against protocol, to tell her they were pulling up anchor.

Polly was distraught and sobbed in her room all morning, while I silently cried for her in my bedroom on the third floor. She seemed so young and vulnerable and couldn't imagine life without Ray.

Mother was trying to run a complicated household with worries about her own sons in the Pacific, and she strove to harness her fears and emotions. Finally, at noon she knocked on Polly's door and said firmly, "Dress, we're going to Schraffts' Restaurant for lunch today." Mother considered Schraffts a sanctuary in times of stress. Polly soon appeared in her suit, hat, and gloves with her eyes so swollen that she could hardly see. Decades later, Polly still expressed appreciation for that lunch and my Mother's tender and understanding gesture that day.

As the war continued, we sought ways we might contribute. The Red Cross and church groups became active in sending CARE packages—Bundles for Britain, then there was Bundles for Breukelen, Holland, for which the Garden Club helped raise funds.

Our friend Nancy Morgan has told us about her Finnish pen pal, Bodil Nordman (a second cousin to Brooklyn Heights' newspaper editor Henrik Krogius). Nancy began to send her outgrown clothes to Bodil: plaid skirts, Shetland sweaters, Mary Jane shoes, smocked dresses, woolen coats, and matching hats. She described her doll collection to Bodil, who said she didn't have a doll and would love one with dark hair. Nancy lined up every doll on her bed, and after serious consideration selected the one to make the journey. She even included an extra outfit. Twelve years later, Nancy and Bodil met for the first time in Finland. Bodil took her upstairs to proudly show her the treasured doll that helped her through the difficult war years and was still sitting serenely in the corner of the room.

One Friday later in the war, the front doorbell rang and Mother was handed a Western Union telegram with the dreaded gold stars on the envelope signifying a death. Louise and I watched with horror as her whole body slumped and began to quake. She strode slowly into the living room and dropped heavily on the sofa. Tears streaked down her face and she shook as she opened it. The message was from a Washington guest expected for dinner the following evening who would not be able to come. The carrier had enclosed it in the wrong type of envelope. It was a mistake! After being so overwhelmed with emotion, Mother then became furious at such carelessness. It was at this moment the war suddenly took on a darker dimension for me. The screaming headlines in the *New York Times* in heavy black print, all those horrid photographs in *LIFE* magazine of fields strewn with dead soldiers in battle dress, of bombings and rubble and ships sinking became real. In that one moment of my mother's terror I

perceived how much stress she was under and how carefully she shielded us from it by striving for normalcy at home while doing all she could for the war effort.

Louise and I cautiously each put an arm around her shoulders in a gesture of comfort. That night I put my favorite teddy bear by her pillow with a verse from a poem by Emily Dickinson. The next day the teddy bear was placed on my bed with a chocolate by his paw, so I assumed he had been of some solace.

Many of the fathers volunteered as air raid wardens and patrolled the streets at night in case bombs fell. One night someone saw a flickering light on the fifteenth floor of a Wall Street building across the East River. This was never allowed because it formed such a visible target. There was much consternation about how to handle it.

The torch in the upraised arm of the Statue of Liberty was even extinguished until the end of the war; we sometimes went down to check it at the foot of Remsen Street.

Some days at noon, sirens mounted on the buildings on Court Street might wail for two minutes. Packer students were assigned by class to move to nearby buildings, which were considered sturdier. I remember walking in orderly rows across the street to the Medical Building, climbing to the fourth floor, and standing in the corridors until the sirens stopped. Being typical students, we welcomed the chance to leave the building and miss some of our classes.

Upper class girls were required to take first aid courses to prepare for emergencies.

The apartment building at 2 Montague Terrace was set up as an air raid station with medicines and food should they be needed.

As the war progressed, busloads of troops were billeted at the St. George Hotel and the streets became packed with sailors in bellbottoms. The Navy Yard was bustling as it shipped out troops bound for Europe. It was impressive to watch a convoy of more than twenty ships depart one after another.

But even these huge departures became commonplace. We all prayed the ships would reach their destination and not be torpedoed by German submarines. Then the ship called the Normandy burned and capsized at its pier on the West Side. There was suspicion of sabotage, which suddenly brought the war close to the Heights. The dangers that had seemed an ocean away were now approaching the Heights.

Servicemen Return Home

From the foot of Montague Street we could see destroyers, PT boats, battleships, and cruisers on the Hudson River. The Queen Mary and Queen Elizabeth II had been converted to troop ships transporting up to three thousand men. Like the others, they were painted battleship gray. We distinguished the familiar ships by their distinct mournful blasts as they slipped into the docks.

Lieutenant Samuel Davidson, one of my favorite cousins, was newly married to Barbara Lasher. Sam had recently graduated from Harvard Medical School and completed a short internship. The newlyweds stayed with us for a month while his convoy waited for overseas departure. Mother put them in the third floor bedroom near mine and I found the newlyweds full of high spirits—off to Atlantic City to swim for the day, off to Roseland where you paid twenty-five cents a dance.

Sam reported to the Brooklyn Navy Yard daily because they were still assembling the convoy and he often returned by noon, or had a day or two off at a time.

Barbara and I walked around the Heights like sisters. I marveled at her enthusiasm over the brownstones, relished our peeking through the wrought-iron fence into Miss White's garden, and our swims in the St. George salt-water pool. As the third week concluded, we knew Sam's departure would be soon. Barbara recalled later, "We were living on the edge, never knowing which

Lt. Samuel Davidson, the author's cousin and newly married to Radcliff graduate Barbara Lasher, saw some hazardous duty as a ship's doctor on convoys traveling the perilous North Atlantic route.

good-bye would be the last."

Sam was one of three doctors assigned to Atlantic convoy duty. They were scheduled to sail north to Belfast, Ireland, then to the Arctic Circle, landing in Murmansk. The convoy consisted of troop ships each holding three thousand men plus Liberty Ships with ammunition, guns, and tanks. The thirty-five ships traveled together, going only as fast as the slowest one. Sam's ship had originally been an Italian luxury liner, the *Conte di Bianco Mano*, and had been gutted of its murals and Circassian walnut paneling. The ships' carpenters sawed up this rare wood to make sea chests for the sailors.

We were thrilled when Sam invited Mother, Louise, and me to visit the ship before departure. We saw the pipe-framed bunks stacked three high. Overcrowding necessitated that men would be assigned different times for their one hour on deck each day. They were served only two meals that were always eaten standing up. We couldn't fathom the claustrophobia and putrid air from seasickness these hardships would entail.

What Louise and I remembered most were the sailors fussing over us; they sent us each off with a whole Hershey chocolate bar and a pack of chewing gum. These were rare items, even in the stores. They suggested, "After you finish chewing a stick of gum, roll it in a ball and put it back in the tin foil. Then place it on the bed and lay down on it. It makes a great back scratcher."

A long time after his return, Sam told us about a call at sea reporting a naval corpsman with acute appendicitis on one of the smaller ships. Sam volunteered to make the transfer from ship-to-ship in the middle of the Atlantic. The whole convoy slowed down as he busily strapped surgical instruments to his body. Then all of his 6-feet 3-inches and 190 pounds were hoisted in a breeches buoy (a contraption that resembled a swing). He was drawn across the water and between the ships by ropes, like traveling on a clothesline.

The seas were angry as he swayed high above the waves and then swooped down to brush the whitecaps before finally landing safely on the other ship's deck.

Down below he ordered the mess table cleared and used it as an operating table. Keeping a steady hand, he completed the operation successfully and the man survived. This was a far cry from the routine complaints of ingrown toenails or VD, which often was contracted after visits in ports where the men visited brothels.

Hosting the newlyweds put my mind on romance. Most of all I wanted to entertain the sailors at the Armory where older Packer girls such as Connie Latson and Betty McKee were allowed to attend Saturday night dances. These events were sponsored by the Red Cross for the servicemen who were about to ship out.

I thought they would be more fun than Miss Hepburn's where you were lucky if a boy danced with you every time. Mother would not be swayed: "You are too young and that is out of the question." I was confident about being a good conversationalist and knew I could cheer up the servicemen. I promised I would never, ever let one kiss me or go outside with one to take a puff on a cigarette. But Mother stood firm.

So I eavesdropped on the upperclassmen at Packer who exchanged whispers and giggles in the halls. According to their stories, they danced to tunes such as "White Christmas" sung by Bing Crosby, and they danced almost nonstop with many sailors cutting in frequently. Rules were strict and everything was orderly. No sailor was ever presumptuous enough to ask for an address.

Still Louise and I were determined to do more. We began writing Victory-mail letters to our brothers, cousins, and some of the young men who had stayed in our guest room. A "V-mail" was written on thin 4¼ by 5-inch pale blue paper that you folded over on dotted lines to make its own envelope and licked to seal. We became convinced our efforts would help to bring our soldiers back safely after the war. Louise and I excitedly opened our return V-mails. Sometimes the censor drew black ink through whole sentences or paragraphs, leaving us to puzzle what special information the writer had tried to convey. Mother and Father urged us to read the letters to the family after dinner. We were surprised at the amount of comfort the soldiers said our letters had afforded.

In the tall windows of the brownstones, more and more white shield banners bordered by red and blue with one or two blue stars began to appear; the stars indicated the number of sons in the service. Roller-skating after school between Pierrepont and Monroe Place with my friend Patty Foote, we noticed a banner with two gold stars arranged vertically in the window; the gold stars signified deaths. We stopped, stunned by this overwhelming loss. I wanted to ring the doorbell and share the family's grief, but not knowing the family, Patty and I decided against it. Some days walking to school was too disturbing; we didn't even look up at the window, afraid more gold stars would be on the banners.

Near the war's end, an overseas package arrived for me from cousin Douggie. It held a sizable piece of his green and black camouflage parachute. The note said, "Dear Alice, This parachute landed me safely behind enemy lines in France and I want you to have it. Your letters saved me from loneliness." No teenager ever had a more prized possession. For a month, I slept with it under my pillow, and I took it to Packer every day with the feeling that I could not be without it.

Finally, the war was over and the servicemen began returning home; there was rejoicing with parades and flags waving. But an inconsolable sadness persisted for a number of our brother's friends, as well as boys from the Heights, who had been killed in action. I noticed and watched with fascination how changed the soldiers' faces were. Many looked strained, some sullen and discouraged. All had lost that youthful burnish and their carefree gait had vanished. Their youth had been snatched away and the deaths would be mourned forever.

Witnessing the end of the war was simultaneously heartbreaking and heartening. We welcomed the new energy as servicemen became decommissioned, discarding uniforms for "civvies," and figuring out what to do next. Some had severe war injuries that altered their future. With the G.I. Bill, many chose to continue their education: high school, college, or graduate school. Some met their children for the first time, those who had been born after they went off to war. There were a flurry of marriages and new families were started. "Rosie the Riveter" and other young women left their jobs so the veterans could step into their places. This became an era when women took pride in staying home, becoming homemakers, and raising their children.

Just as families embarked on the never-ending process of grieving, so they also rejoiced in safe returns and the arrival of tiny new faces—the first members of the baby boom generation.

Leaving Remsen Street

Mother and Father had moved to 82 Remsen Street in 1936 after Grandfather and Grandmother Hooker had died. Now the years had progressed into the mid-1950s, and Mother's arthritis had become more of a problem and the house had far more space then she and Father needed. Bessie and Nora were still there, but all six children were now married and raising families in their own homes elsewhere. Day after day, week after week, our family debated selling 82 Remsen Street.

Mother was determined to move before her health failed, and was confident she could create a new smaller home in Brooklyn Heights. Father knew it made sense to move to smaller quarters but he was reluctant to go. Father was emotionally attached to our home and was unable to picture himself elsewhere. This had been his first real home: six children had been raised here and it embodied the history of his adult life. Because Father and his brothers were sent away to boarding school as children and stayed with cousins on vacations, he had not experienced the security of a his own regular home until he was married.

Father had been master of our unusual and handsome Remsen Street house for twenty-one years. There was so much he loved: the richness of the oak paneling and the large oil paintings throughout the downstairs. Many had been purchased at the Paris Exposition over the decades. The

The front entrance of 82 Remsen Street.

graceful wide oak staircases went right up to the third floor, and there were ample places for his grandfather clocks. He always looked forward to reading the Sunday *New York Times* after church in the sunny conservatory with the light flooding over ferns and blooming plants. The almost tropical setting contrasted to the darker oak paneled living room beyond. And sizable dinner parties and evening receptions had become part of Mother and Father's yearly rituals.

This fireplace at 82 Remsen Street had been copied from one at Knole Castle in England.

And what about those magnificent Oriental rugs? They were far too expansive for any smaller space…although on closer inspection they were indeed worn. And what about the larger pieces of furniture that would look out of scale? Father never played the Steinway piano but enjoyed seeing its sturdy frame at the end of the living room; none of the children had shown any musical promise despite years of lessons from patient teachers. No regular-sized apartment would accommodate the stacks of beautiful china or cut-glass goblets residing in those dining room cabinets that reached to the ceiling. Surely, the carved oak dining room table and chairs Grandfather Hooker had commissioned from Philadelphia craftsmen would have to be left behind. And the Tudor oak sideboard that held the flat silverware would have to go. As patriarch of the household Father relished standing at the head of the table to carve the Sunday roast beef while Bessie passed the vegetables

"Now, Sid" Mother said, "Nine bedrooms, as many baths, and three floors plus a full basement is ridiculous for us now. I feel overwhelmed running this house. The arthritis in my knees is worse and some days I can hardly manage the stairs. We need something more practical."

Help to maintain the house also was becoming more difficult to hire; the large pool of Irish immigrant girls seeking household employment no longer existed. Bessie and Nora remained with Mother and Father but were growing older and were not as nimble as they used to be. Nor was the man who arrived promptly at 9 a.m. Monday mornings to adjust the timepieces. Mrs. Joyce, who cleaned for years, had retired and no satisfactory replacement had been found. The laundress had long since gone. Mother did not like compromising her standards and was not going to run the house at half speed.

Once Father realized Mother was serious about moving, he agreed to look at apartments. They both wanted to stay in the neighborhood and hoped for a view of the East River. To our delight and without much fuss, they agreed on a place at One Pierrepont Street. The apartment, with its high ceilings and nicely proportioned rooms, had a view over the East River and was ample—but could almost have fit on the first floor of 82 Remsen Street. Together they made decisions on which furniture and paintings would fit the scale of the apartment and decided how each would be placed. A few items were purchased at the Parke Bernet auction house.

Slowly but surely, Father let go of his daily rituals. Although he would be in the same neighborhood and still walk the Brooklyn Bridge to Wall Street with his friends of long standing, he would no longer go down that handsome stoop at 82 Remsen Street. Instead, he would push the button in an elevator and walk onto the sidewalk. Still, at the new location there was a view of the East River and the harbor that was certainly desirable. He had always enjoyed watching the panorama of ferryboats and activity on the waterfront from the foot of Remsen Street.

Mother started her moving project with the carriage house, which had never been completely cleared out after Grandfather died. It had become a repository for everything large that didn't fit into the main house. The building was filled with accumulated piles of nowhere-else-to-put things. Armed with her formidable organizational skills, as well as her notebook and pencil, Mother walked across the garden every morning after breakfast and opened the creaky door to the carriage house. She commenced to categorize the items and decide where they should go.

There was an odd assortment: the slate chemistry counters from Grandfather Hooker's research days, boxes of beakers and other equipment left behind after the lab had been sold, worn-out leather armchairs from his study, old radios, even toys from our childhood… She paused in Grandfather's theater on the second floor, remembering his unforgettable magic shows for audiences of fellow magicians in the early 1900s. The men were always dressed formally in black tie; they all sat on folding chairs as the red velvet curtain parted.

The famous rising bear head, Miltiades, once had baffled all the magicians by opening and shutting his mouth the correct number of times to identify numbers on playing cards. Militates had been packed away in twenty boxes. The instructions about assembling him and his secrets remained in the rusted safe. Grandfather had not wanted his secrets to die with him, nor did he wish them published.

As a teenager, my brother Bob had mastered a modest repertoire of magic tricks; he agreed to take charge of finding a proper home for Miltiades. His search was to last two decades before the bear head was finally passed on to a younger magician who had known Grandfather.

The next task was to scale back furnishings and to see which family items each of the six adult children would want in their own homes. That Thanksgiving of 1958, we all were summoned for our last celebration in the house. We each were given stickers to put on our favorite pieces and paintings that were not going to the new apartment. My husband John and I were busy settling into academic life at the University of Vermont in Burlington and starting our family. I chose three items from my bedroom: the slant top Queen Ann maple desk where I settled down to study each evening, the maple bureau with brass pulls, and Queen Anne mirror. I also took the handsome grandfather clock from the second floor that had chimed the hours through my childhood.

The one collectible item I coveted was an unusual Staffordshire hen of Grandfather's

that Mother brought out every Easter. She was of white china with etched feathers and a red comb. When Mother took off the lid, multi-colored jellybeans and Easter eggs hid in green grass. Remarkably, no one else seemed to want her, and she remains my prize today in our dining room among other Staffordshire animals we have collected.

I thought it would be difficult to bid goodbye to 82 Remsen Street, but by that Thanksgiving the furnishings were disassembled and it looked so different. My sister Louise and I knew we would miss the dumbwaiter, which symbolized our childhood and all the amusement we had pulling it up and down, or occasionally climbing on the shelves for hide-and-seek games. There was always the delight of Nora's steaming dishes drawn up to the pantry to be carried in to the dining room table by Bessie.

Meanwhile, my parents' worn chairs were redone or replaced, as were some Oriental rugs. Paint colors and lovely fabrics were chosen for the windows and upholstery. These often picked up the colors in the oil paintings and gave a pleasing quality to each room. Father became quite engaged in this planning; he wanted a traditional feel with some grandeur, while still surrounded by his favorite pieces. The results were stunning.

After the movers had left and the house had been cleaned, Father closed the door for the last time and followed Mother out. Arm in arm they walked down the stoop, never looking back.

"My Cup Runneth Over"

We were all amazed at how easily Mother and Father settled into their new apartment at One Pierrepont Street. They enjoyed friends of all ages, such as Tristan, Bertel and Eleanor Antell, and Lewis Francis who lived on various floors. I wondered if this move to the apartment might resemble a college community with friends dropping in helter-skelter to sit cross-legged on the Oriental rugs for long pow-wows. But this definitely was not the case. Father and Mother were still able to maintain their privacy.

The convenience of being on one floor with no stairs was greater than they had anticipated. The superintendent was available to fix leaky faucets and endless pesky things. The amiable Irish doorman sent them off as they left and greeted them on return.

The apartment somewhat resembled the feel of 82 Remsen Street with their favorite paintings, antique furniture, and Oriental rugs. Everything was freshly painted and the oak paneling had been traded for a sunnier, more up-to-date look. It was as if they had been transported into the twentieth century.

Mother had acquired two prize additions: one was a French tapestry dating to the mid-1700s, which hung on the dining room wall. Its intricate needlepoint was stitched by hand with a forest motif of birds and flowers, a piece of museum quality. Each time I examined it I found some new detail I had missed. The other prize additions were

A photograph of the author's parents. The couple happily continued to preside over family celebrations from their new apartment at One Pierrepont Street.

the dining room table and chairs that had belonged to the Duke of Leeds in England, purchased from an auction at Sotheby's. These made her feel connected to Grandfather Hooker's English heritage.

Half the dining room table was situated by the window and connected only for larger groups. Each half comfortably accommodated six people, which meant Mother and Father weren't sitting at the enormously long oak table at 82 Remsen Street with room for ten.

Mother presiding over Thanksgiving dinner at the Pierrepont Street apartment.

Bessie loved her plants and placed them in the sun on the other table. They flourished under her care, giving an illusion of the Remsen Street house's conservatory.

The dumbwaiter was a thing of the past. Nora cooked their food, heated Father's dinner plates, and Bessie brought meals through the small pantry into the dining room. Even the door made the same quiet swoosh as she passed through followed by a few delicious fragrances. Everything was to scale, making the apartment appear larger. The overall ambiance was one of quiet elegance, comfort, and relaxation.

Celebrating Thanksgiving proved the real trial run as Mother and Father wanted all the children and grandchildren in attendance. There was only one guest room so most of us stayed at the Yale Club in New York and came over by subway. Two college age grandchildren did walk the Brooklyn Bridge and reported it as an impressive feat. They could hardly believe their Grandfather still strode daily to his Wall Street office.

There were twenty-eight of us that day. Mother had two folding coat racks she had purchased at Altman's set up in the hallway, handy as we emerged from the elevator. We had sherry in the study overlooking the East River. To seat us all Bessie had set up seven card tables in the living room with the familiar white initialed linen napkins, the flat silver, and flower arrangements.

Best of all, Father carved the forty-pound turkey at the head of the table portioning out the drum sticks, second joints, white and dark meat, with ample dollops of Nora's stuffing, just as he had done in the past. Mother's favorite creamed onions were in the silver dish next to the candied sweet potatoes and fluffy rice. He beamed as he surveyed his family gathered all around him once again.

I observed two of the name cards had been switched and later found out one of the younger grandchildren, Leecie, had done that because she wanted to be with the grown-ups, not at the "baby table" with her age group. I regularly tried this very same trick at age ten but never got away with it; then the "baby table" was in the conservatory rather than the dining room, so I was promptly sent right back to where I belonged. Conversely, Leecie assured me the adults liked having her with them and that she kept up her end of the conversation well.

All the women and girls of our family noticed small festive presents by their places. Father had gone to Harry Winston, the jeweler, and worked with the head designer. He ordered handsome individual gold pins, designed with each of our initials entwined to remember the occasion. The men and boys got handsome Italian silk ties. He presented Mother with a gorgeous flower pin: sapphire petals on a platinum stem, each with a diamond in the middle. Harry Winston rarely made gold pins to order; the company was known for its unusual designs incorporating large gemstones. We were surprised at Father's extravagance and great generosity to all. He had never done anything like this before; he usually went to Tiffany's for Mother's special occasion jewelry.

Father then gave a toast to Mother: "You know how reluctant I was to leave our home, the first real home I ever had. But in your wisdom, you realized the time to move had come. I thank you from the bottom of my heart, Al, for your foresight and for this past year of hard work that made all of this possible. I love our new home, which is so special and comfortable and far easier for us both. My cup runneth over."

Epilogue

BESSIE'S LAST DAYS

As time passed, it became clearer that Mother, Father, Bessie, and Nora, although healthy, were no longer energetic. At One Pierrepont Street Bessie was assigned a smaller bedroom with the same furniture, although Mother re-covered the armchair in gay flowered chintz. Bessie's cross and picture of Jesus were hung on the wall as before. It disturbed me that her tiny room was just off the kitchen, which seemed like an affront. However, Bessie told me she preferred the arrangement because she no longer had to climb to the third floor. She could also slip down the back stairs and chat with the Irish doorman, who kept her up on apartment gossip.

Mrs. Outwater, my mother-in-law, was a frequent dinner guest and Bessie, who admired her, looked forward to her visits. Mrs. Outwater dressed elegantly in clothes from London and Paris shops; she usually brought Bessie a carefully wrapped present from her travels. When Mrs. Outwater died, my husband John and I were sorting out her clothes when he suggested we take some to Bessie, who seemed about the same size. I scooped up several dresses, a dressing gown, matching slippers, two fur-trimmed coats with matching hats, handbags, a couple of pairs of cashmere-lined leather gloves, and at the last minute—why not?—a few bottles of her French perfume.

To my relief, Bessie was thrilled with the bounty and immediately began hanging the clothes in her closet.

"Do you think you will ever wear them?" I asked nervously.

"Oh, yes indeed. I have a wedding and a confirmation coming up soon," she replied.

Bessie tried on the navy blue satin French dressing gown splashed with gay flowers, put on the slippers, and then shyly turned this way and that to admire herself in the mirror.

"Bessie, you look gorgeous," I remarked.

The next week I saw her slip out the door wearing one of Mrs. Outwater's coats—

but with her old handbag and no hat, as if testing how it felt. A few Saturdays later, when I was there again visiting from Vermont, I looked out the window and saw the doorman smartly tipping his hat to her as she left in Mrs. Outwater's taupe coat with mink collar and the fur-trimmed hat cocked jauntily on the side of her head. The outfit was complete with leather gloves and French handbag. Bessie walked with assurance and even had a spring in her step. I had not noticed how saucy and slim her ankles were, although I imagine the doorman had appreciated them long ago.

The next morning Bessie said, "Oh, the grand time I had at my niece's wedding! Everyone commented on my outfit and the print silk dress. They wanted to know where I had gotten such fine clothes. My nephew even danced with me."

Gradually Bessie became more outgoing and relaxed as if the responsibilities of raising children were over and she felt a release. She still had some good years left and was now going to indulge in a few adventures. During this period, Mother and Father also branched out with trips to India, Egypt, and Angkor Wat as well as taking several cruises.

While they were away, Bessie looked after the apartment but was not strictly on duty. This was a new experience for her after years of being on an unrelenting schedule, catering to our full household at 82 Remsen Street.

One Friday Bessie seemed uncharacteristically excited: she mentioned that she had visited Atlantic City with her cousin. Together they had walked the Boardwalk and even gambled. Bessie had won $100, an enormous sum at the time. I nudged her for more details, but Bessie turned to finish the dusting; her secret was no one's business but her own.

Bessie was nearing eighty when I began to notice how uneasy and worried she seemed. Her energy was lessening and she wanted to retire in the Pierrepont House run by Catholic Charities, just up from Mother and Father's apartment. The building was handsome and considered one of the best run Catholic retirement homes around. Many of Bessie's friends were living there, and that was where she felt she belonged. This request involved a complicated process of applications, waiting lists, and interviews. A year of frustration passed with no headway, and so she asked my brother Bob to help her, the only time I can recall her asking for any favors.

During this time, Father had died and Mother was very reluctant to have Bessie leave because her own health was failing too. Bessie had been part of Mother's tapestry for decades and essential to her natural order of things.

Nevertheless, after all these years of service to the family, Bessie deserved a few years of leisure. Finally, she was accepted at Pierrepont House and she acquired a sunny apartment on the ninth floor. If she leaned out the window, she got a similar view of the East River and the Statue of Liberty as our family had at One Pierrepont Street. Bessie joyously moved in to take her place among her own.

She became somewhat of a celebrity there. Bessie's domain had been the pantry and first floor at 82 Remsen Street, now she surfaced at the top of the Pierrepont House hierarchy, and was looked up to by other residents. Her consideration and acceptance of others meant that she got along easily with everyone. As always, Bessie handled herself with straightforwardness and grace.

Her retirement home had a number of activities for the residents. Bessie now could enjoy her favorable financial situation. She was a regular at teatime (served by someone else), became an avid Bingo player, and took trips to Atlantic City with her friends, but told me, "I never gamble; my luck might turn and I'd lose money."

The one sadness was my Mother's lack of adjustment to the rupture in her world when Bessie left. Mother was in a wheelchair by now; nurses and helpers came and went but the apartment was not as crisply run as before. Mother viewed this as shockingly makeshift, an unsatisfactory arrangement after having run her household with great skill for decades.

My siblings, the grandchildren, and I visited as regularly as we could. Mother only minimally welcomed Bessie, which must have been painful for both. Instead, Bessie telephoned weekly to inquire how Mother was doing. I felt sadness about the rift between such steadfastly proud elderly women.

Mother had always stressed the importance of appropriate manners and treating others well no matter what their station. As she reached her nineties, her mental landscape became fuzzy and she could not seem to follow these guideposts. Mother died at ninety-five in 1984 and Bessie sat beside us at the funeral in the First Unitarian Church.

John, our children, and I continued telephoning Bessie from Vermont to share our family news and most of all to hear her Irish brogue waft through the phone. Bessie became very frail at ninety-one. In the midst of a snowstorm she reported, "Miss Alice, the snowflakes are coming down on the window panes like baseballs. And the maidenhair fern has just been repotted."

"Did you get your Christmas present, Bessie?" I asked.

"Oh, thank you, Miss Alice, but I've had the same bath towels for seven years and they are still fine."

"But Bessie, these are blue, your favorite color, and so thick and fuzzy. I had them monogrammed at Altman's with your initials, just like Mother's always were."

"Thank you, Miss Alice, yes, I'll use them and give the others away. You have always been so good thinking of me."

"Bessie, I love you so much," I said in reply. And the phone clicked off. Bessie was never one to talk for long. That was our last conversation. Bessie died that snowy night.

Acknowledgements

I am indebted to all of my teachers at Packer Collegiate Institute and Vassar College who loved their subjects and bestowed in me the exhilaration of learning. To David Huddle at the University of Vermont, whose undergraduate writing course I took two years in a row. A gifted teacher, he wanted us all to be writers.

Linda Bland has been editing my pieces for several years. She has been patient and quietly encouraging, serious but lighthearted; she has straightened out my tangled grammar, sometimes even clarifying my thoughts.

Henrik Krogius, the editor of the *Brooklyn Heights Press,* published each one of my stories over a period of five years. He treated them tenderly as he skillfully captioned and placed the photos. Henrik even took camera in hand to take additional photographs of the neighborhood.

The team of people at Wind Ridge Publishing offered support in many ways: Lin Stone, Laurie Thomas, Kathy Howard, Nancy Warren, and Holly Johnson each shared their skills and resources and consistently demonstrated their belief in my work.

Many family members and friends boosted me throughout this endeavor: my four children, Anne, Catherine, Alice, and John

The author's children: Anne, Johnny, Catherine, Alice.

III; Bob, Louise, and Don Heyneman; Edie, Caleb, Susan, Mary, Tres, Anne, David, and Treat; Sarah, Pat, Chris and Helen; Jonathan and Amy; Pat, Carol, Biri, Dag Berntsen in Norway; Myra and Eric; Carl, Josie, and Hank; Lydia and Jackson; Ynez and Mel; Oda; Eleanor in Alaska; Ginger; Gay; Peter; Kate and Bill; Elise; Jeannie; Luisa; Janet; Libby and Molly King; and not to overlook Bill Rust, who dashed over frequently to handle glitches in my computer.

And to my beloved late husband of 56 years, John Ogden Outwater, Jr., thank you for being my champion and unabashedly delighting in my successes and achievements. You are forever by my side.

I am grateful to all, including those not mentioned, and hope you enjoy reading my reminiscences.

Reading Group Discussion Questions

CLASS AND CULTURE

1. Describe the boundaries drawn between the household staff and the Davidson family. Were they enforced? What was the relationship of Mrs. Davidson to the household staff?
2. What responsibilities did Mr. and Mrs. Davidson assume on behalf of the household staff? Was this unusual for the period? Would it be unusual today?
3. Comment on the sense of duty and integrity the help exhibited, including the people who came in for particular jobs, i.e. laundress, coal man, etc. Was trustworthiness and honesty assumed and more prevalent than today? (The coal man had keys for every single house on the block…) Think of other contrasting examples of trust from the stories and today.
4. Describe the bond between the author and Bebe, her nursemaid, and Bessie, the upstairs maid.
5. What was Ireland's economic situation in the 1920s and 1930s when so many people were emigrating? Do you think that the immigrants were welcome here?

Is it likely that they encountered prejudice and if so, how did they respond? To what extent did the immigrants incorporate aspects of their home country to their identity in the United States? What role did the priest and Catholic Church play in the life of the maids?

6. How have the lives of Irish people and their status in this country changed in the past 70 years?
7. Did your own ancestors have struggles as immigrants in America? How were they similar to or different from the Irish immigrant experience?

FAMILY LIFE

1. Given the privileged nature of their childhoods, would you consider the author or her siblings spoiled? What Davidson family luxuries or indulgences surprised you? Did you find any frugalities, and if so, did you think them prudent? What are comparable luxuries today?

2. Does it seem unusual that the author's maternal and paternal grandparents lived across the street from one another

and got along well together? Did their interests and lifestyles differ? Was this proximity among families more common in this era? In what ways might it have been beneficial?

3. Mr. Davidson was a Victorian father and imposed strict rules on the children. Why did they accept those rules so willingly? Would this be true today? How has child rearing changed?

4. Did children have more or less freedom and independence then? Why? Did neighbors and friends play a role in child safety then? Do they play that role now?

5. What was the importance of family rituals? What new family rituals do we have now and what older traditions have persisted? What purpose did the parties and entertaining play in the family and community? How do parties differ today?

6. It was assumed the author and her siblings would graduate from Vassar and Yale; each of the children had a summer abroad with the Experiment in International Living before attending college; additionally, the daughters were expected to work for a year before marrying. Comment on these expectations and the lack of individual choice. Was this a reflection on the family, class, or the times? What are today's expectations for daughters? Sons? Why do you think their parents required this?

War and Memories

1. When the United States was bombed by Japan and entered WWII, siblings and cousins dropped out of college and signed up for service in droves. Why was the majority of the population so willing to do this?

2. What changes did the author note in these stories as part of the aftermath of war?

3. When servicemen went to war, many women stepped up and into the workforce (think "Rosie the Riveter"); when the servicemen returned, women stepped aside, went home, and became the 1950's housewives who gave birth to the "baby boom generation." Comment on how this might have framed society's views on mothering, women's roles, and the workplace.

4. How does this memoir differ from others that focus on childhood memories (*Angela's Ashes* or the *Glass Castle,* for example)? What details in the stories help you picture life in the 1930s and 1940s?

5. Which story did you like the best? Why? Is it important to learn about everyday life from previous eras?